The GRACE GIVING leader

PRAISE FOR THE GRACE-GIVING LEADER

Jan's passion is inspiring, her leadership is proven, and the wisdom she shares in *The Grace-Giving Leader* will set you on a path to living a life of impact for God's Kingdom.

Best-selling author, Founder of Propel Women & A21—CHRISTINE CAINE

For more than a decade I've had the privilege of watching Jan Greenwood empower and equip women. Her faithfulness and consistency have left an indelible mark on me and thousands of others. When she prays, the depth of her intimacy with Jesus shines through. When she teaches, the Scriptures are sharp on her tongue. When she writes, the heartfelt sentiments of her soul shimmer on each and every page. And when she leads, her influence is punctuated with a grace that is reflective of the One whom she has given her life to serve. I'm so grateful for Jan's ministry and, after reading *The Grace-Giving Leader*, I know you will be too.

Author and Bible Teacher—PRISCILLA SHIRER

It is rare to find someone who speaks to the soul of leadership the way Jan Greenwood does. In *The Grace-Giving Leader*, Jan imparts years of wisdom, experience, and skill that will equip you to lead with strength and grace. Jan will challenge you with thought-provoking concepts, and she will also guide you through the process of understanding the impact of your short-term leadership decisions on the long-term impact of a life lived well. If you are committed to serving God and his people, Jan is the right woman to help you grow your gift of influencing the kingdom of God by shepherding others with excellence.

Bible teacher, Author, Founder of The Sister Circle—CHRYSTAL EVANS HURST

In *The Grace-Giving Leader,* Jan continues her passion to speak into and mentor others on their journey of leadership elevation with her practical examples and priceless pearls with which I implore you to adorn yourself. Please don't just read *The Grace-Giving Leader,* consume it, all the while pausing and pondering how to apply it personally. It will make a difference to you in whatever and wherever you are in your individual sphere of leadership and influence.

CEO, Corporate Director, Co-host of *The Leader's Panel* Podcast—LORIANN BIGGERS

I highly endorse *The Grace-Giving Leader* and the phenomenal leader who authored it. Jan Greenwood is a treasured mentor and friend. She lives grace-filled and leads accordingly. It is a joy to learn from her, and I know *The Grace-Giving Leader* will be a resource I refer to for years to come.

Women's Pastor, Gateway Church Southlake Campus—JEN WEAVER

Many influencers want to impact the masses, but they bypass the inner-work necessary to lead well. *The Grace-Giving Leader* includes time-tested secrets to equip and empower you, from trusted-mentor and proven leader, Jan Greenwood. Discover how to effectively lead yourself and others through the wisdom of Scripture, the power of grace, and reflection questions that will move you forward in maturity.

Pastor's Wife at Central Church, Speaker, Author, Mom of Five—KATIE M. REID

The Grace-Giving Leader is a brilliant wake-up call for leaders on how to use the concept of grace as a key to power. She lives what she preaches: Grace can take your limited experience, resources, vision and influence and propel you to greater wholeness, health and real leadership success. This is a beautiful and empowering book that will inspire every leader.

President and Co-founder of Embrace Grace—AMY FORD

PRAISE FOR THE GRACE-GIVING LEADER

This book is a prescription for leaders desiring to lead effectively and powerfully with grace. Jan Greenwood walks out these words as she leads and mentors those around her. Grace is the language she lives by and this book is a telling of how that grace came to be in her life and how we too can be grace-giving leaders ourselves. If you lead in any capacity this book will challenge your thinking on what leadership is and should be and how we need to give and receive grace.

Author, Speaker, Founder of Brave Moms—KRISTIN LEMUS

There are so many things I love about *The Grace-Giving Leader*. The insights and advice in these pages are life lessons we all need. The personal stories are authentic and vulnerable yet reveal Jan's strength and God-anointed leadership giftings - so rare to find in a book for women! This is really going to resonate and equip a lot of women to lead in a more spiritually powerful, effective and fulfilling way!"

Leadership Consultant, Speaker, Author—KADI COLE

Each page of *The Grace-Giving Leader* beckons you to turn another. Jan Greenwood has fought hard to comprehend the grace she writes of and walks in it beautifully. She is a cheerleader, prayer warrior, strategic thinker, exhorter, and friend to many. Her vulnerability will encourage and impact all women. The stories she shares are easily applied to any woman's life, no matter the age.

Pastor of Strategies, Conferences and Events, Gateway Church—MALLORY BASSHAM

In the era of reality TV and Social Media, we find an emerging generation starving for authenticity. *The Grace-Giving Leader* delivers that yearned for authenticity. Over the years I have been inspired by the graceful way in which Jan Greenwood sailed through seemingly impossible leadership situations. To know her up close only confirmed what I guessed at from a distance: She is authentic, joyful, wise, humble, and full of grace. May you treasure every word as you go on your own grace-giving journey.

Founding Associate Pastor, Covenant Church, Author—AMIE HAYES DOCKERY

The Grace-Giving Leader will not only impact you; it will impact the leaders you are raising up. I know firsthand that Jan Greenwood personally lives out what she teaches in this book. When Jan came into my life years ago, she taught me these very principles that were life changing for me.

Pastor of Summit Women, Founder of She Is Conference—KIM MASENGALE

In *The Grace-Giving Leader,* Jan Greenwood challenges women to speak wisdom and grace into any situation. Jan consistently lives out what she shares as she uses her ability to mentor the people God places in front of her in any season of life and empower them forward. *The Grace-Giving Leader* is an effective resource for any leader (new or seasoned) containing practical tools that when used will ensure your success as you learn to lead others.

Next Steps Pastor, Beltway Church—DEANNA FIELDS

I love *The Grace-Giving Leader* and the empowerment of women to walk in the unforced rhythms of GRACE for ourselves and others. Jan is a dear friend. She is strategic, prophetic, wise, and a wonderful leader. It is humbling that she chose Grace to be the reigning quality. We need this! This is how God operates and we should to. As you read *The Grace-Giving Leader* make sure to leave room for your heart to expand in the most beautiful ways.

Groups Pastor, Gateway Church Southlake Campus—STEPHANIE KELSEY

Jan Greenwood is one of those mentors with a precious way of sitting with you and reminding you of truth even as you dig up roots you may not even realize have taken hold of the tender places in your heart. In *The Grace-Giving Leader,* Jan gently reminds you to focus less on the title of your call and focus more on the one who called you in the first place! She reminds you that God has chosen you, He has had His eye on you, and He wants you to experience His grace so that you can extend it to others. And isn't that the most important call of all?

Women's Minister, The Hills Church—BARBARA GRADKE

PRAISE FOR THE GRACE-GIVING LEADER

The Grace-Giving Leader is an honest expedition inside the lives of leaders with feet of clay and hearts of gold. Between these pages, you'll find yourself—your ambitions and dreams, your struggles and setbacks, even your frustrations and disappointments. You will find incredible encouragement and practical wisdom. If you have a tenacious belief in the best version of who God created you to be, and you refuse to live your life aimlessly beneath the vision of God's highest plans, then *The Grace-Giving Leader* is the right book for you.

Author, Publisher, Motivational Speaker—WENDY K. WALTERS

The Grace-Giving Leader is such an excellent resource for all regardless of place, position, or pace. Jan takes you into the material and prompts you to think deeper about leading with grace. She has thoughtfully compiled a variety of perspectives that highlight various journeys making this a delightful, yet powerful resource. You will grow as a result.

Founder of Cassie Reid Counseling and Church Rehab
Director of Marriage and Family Therapy, The King's University—DR. CASSIE REID

In *The Grace-Giving Leader,* you'll find the grace-filled mentor you've been hoping to find in your own journey as a leader. Jan Greenwood shares her wisdom through personal stories, extensive research, and hard-won experience… and then like the generous leader she is, she highlights others and gives space for their leadership stories. Jan weaves a handbook of leadership principles with the skill and tender care of a mentor's mentor: an unwavering champion of the gifts within you--so that you can become the effective, powerful and grace-giving leader you are called to be.

Speaker, Artist, Author—RACHEL ANNE RIDGE

The Grace-Giving Leader is a principle I have been honored to learn in sitting under Jan Greenwood's leadership. Jan exudes grace in all that she does in life and ministry. Without her leadership, I would not be the woman I am today. I am thrilled this resource is now available to women all over the world.

Speaker, Counselor, Host of *Real Talk with Rachael*— RACHAEL GILBERT

We are a society that's continually inundated with information and advice on how to be a better, stronger, and more successful leader. *The Grace-Giving Leader.* is truly a breath, a pause, and a reflective, contemplative step away from the 'noise' and into the truth about what it means to lead with integrity, grace, and a heart for Christ. As she unpacks difficult moments of her life with honesty and clarity, she reflects the importance of leading with humility—something that is so often overlooked in our aim-to-please culture. This book is a blessing to all who read it. I am thankful to know Jan and her truly selfless, servant heart."

Writer, Coach, Founder of Be A Light Collective—MARISA DONNELLY

"If you are even entertaining the idea of leadership, *The Grace-Giving Leader* is a MUST HAVE!!! This precious gal has been leading and launching leaders throughout her calling to serve women —and applying her wisdom and encouragement will take YOUR leadership opportunities to greater grace-filled heights! Get ready to make a difference in your spheres of influence!"

Bible Teacher, Author—LEEANN KIRKINDOLL

In *The Grace-Giving Leader*, Jan not only supports and renews your hope, she helps you regain vision from the Lord, reflect on His will, and increase your leadership skills. God brought Jan into my life when I was in an uncertain waiting season. Jan not only supported and renewed my hope, she helped me regain vision from the Lord, reflect on His will, and increase in knowledge on a leadership virtue. Her love, her joy and her grace are contagious! I am so glad you will come to know my dear friend Jan Greenwood. I am confident she will bless your leadership in the same magnitude that she has blessed mine!

Leader, Prophetic Intercessor, Founder of Prayerful Signs—AMBER COLBERG

What better person to write about grace-giving than one of the most gracious leaders of our day? In *The Grace-Giving Leader,* Jan Greenwood's timely leadership insights leave a legacy that will equip you to lead in a safe, loving, and empowering manner that always brings out the best in others and ourselves.

Educator, Speaker, Author—MARILYN WEIHER

In *The Grace-Giving Leader,* Jan Greenwood parts ways with the contemporary approach of platform building to, instead, mentor and raise up godly and grace-filled leaders. Transparent, conversational, and life-giving, Jan uplifts a diverse set of voices across the board of Christian female leaders, articulating the grace needed to properly impart leadership. If you are looking for a safe place to wrestle through the challenging seasons of leadership on your way to God's greater calling, you've found it.

Speaker, Author, Co-founder of Now Found Publishing—COURTNEY COHEN

Jan Greenwood is the epitome of the title of this book. She is one of the most grace-giving leaders I know. In *The Grace-Giving Leader,* you are called to be a leader in the sphere God gives us, but not just any type of leader, a leader who follows God's model of grace-filled leadership and walks humbly alongside others. Jan shares beautifully how we can all walk in this type of leadership.

Senior Manager, Global Child Development Ministry—STEPHANIE THOMPSON

The Grace-Giving Leader is a timely message to grow Godly women into roles that shape the course of history. In her newest book Jan challenges us to pursue a level of leadership that goes beyond the ordinary to fulfill God dreams! Jan's life experiences and her journey with the Lord compel us to deeply love and tenderly raise up a new generation of strong, gracious, life-giving women.

Bible Teacher, Author, Gateway Church, Jackson Hole—SHEREE HALL

The Grace-Giving Leader struck a chord in my performance-driven heart. Jan Greenwood takes us on a journey to find the grace of God that was always available. I've learned to lean into grace and to trust the dream that God has given me. Experiencing The Grace-Giving Leader was like holding a mirror up to my face, reminding me that God is bigger than my dreams - my job is to lead with grace and trust Him. This book will challenge you, inspire you and move you into powerful grace-filled leadership.

Speaker, Touring Director for Compassion LIVE, Podcast Host—MARY R SNYDER

The power of the message found in *The Grace-Giving Leader* is that Jan wholeheartedly lives it out in her own life. The secrets that she unpacks come from real life experiences and testing. Here you will find the perfect combination of grace and truth. Welcome to a new leadership journey full of empowerment that will help you go boldly in the direction God is calling you."

Leader, Advisory Team Lead with Brave Strong Girl—EMILY MILLER

In *The Grace-Giving Leader,* Jan holds nothing back. She will be your biggest cheerleader and encounter while pointing you to God. This book is more than just another book on leadership. It's relational and laced with divine revelation and authority under the Holy Spirit, that will position every leader to live and serve by grace and not perfection. Each chapter ends with questions to "pause & ponder". You will be captivated with an up-close personal look into Jan's heart and her vision, while gently pointing you to God's Word and the importance of always seeking His presence and wisdom.

Businesss Professional, Advisory Team Lead with Brave Strong Girl—RHONDA LOVE

One of the most valuable of lessons I learned from *The Grace-Giving Leader* is how giving AND receiving grace can change a situation, an attitude, a heart in a single moment, not just as a leader in ministry or work but in the home, in relationships and friendships as well.

Founder of Stunningly Strong—GENA BOHL

Right now, our world deeply needs "grace extenders". In *The Grace-Giving Leader,* Jan Greenwood powerfully and eloquently encourages leaders to allow the Holy Spirit to take the helm of their lives, using the compass of truth, towards the direction of grace. Transforming!

Prophetic Evangelist, Intercessor, Bible Teacher— KRISTIN PASCHKE

This is such a critical time in history for followers of Jesus to wake up and rise up to His command to lead in every sector of culture. Jan Greenwood reminds us that every believer is a leader. *The Grace-Giving Leader* will challenge you, affirm you, and prepare you from the inside out for your Kingdom assignment.

Leader, Bible Teacher—ROBYN BRINKLEY,

I will forever be impacted by *The Grace-Giving Leader* and will recommend it as a resource to everyone I know. Pastor Jan has been one of the most profound and instrumental leaders and mentors in my life these past few years. As a leader and mentor, I'm able to relate to similar experiences she's had, like some of the hardest, yet most beneficial lessons we learn on our journey to become a respected, successful leader. Her words of wisdom, and assurance of who my identity came from, and learning to trust where God was taking me, changed my thought processes to the core.

Leader, Mentor, Chaplain—VELINDA BUCHANAN

This is not just another book about grace. It is grace demonstrated through so many different lives. No matter what season you are in, *The Grace-Giving Leader* will speak to you. Grace! Such a great gift! This spoke to me in each and every chapter. Jan teaches and unlocks the refreshing lessons of Grace. No matter what season you are in, you'll find new grace awaits.

Leader, Business Professional—NANETTE EILAND

The Grace-Giving Leader are packed full of empowering stories that can't help but ignite a renewed passion for serving God in our roles and expanding our capacity to excitedly love the way Jesus has called us to love! You just can't help but feel empowered to face whatever challenges are before you. Jan warmly invites us to join her on the journey to discovering God's purpose for grace in all areas of our lives, especially the areas where we are leading and serving others.

Leader, Bible Teacher—LORETTA MOERBE

Are you ready to heal from hurtful leaders, be set free, and become a Grace-Giving Leader, empowered by the Holy Spirit for healthy ministry? Then *The Grace-Giving Leader* is the book for you. Through this book, Jan Greenwood has helped me overcome my fears of leading poorly, and empowered me to step into my God-given leadership roles with joy.

Real Estate Agent, Missionary, Pastor's Wife, Advisory Team Lead with Brave Strong Girl—JESSICA REED

FOREWORD BY HOLLY WAGNER

the GRACE GIVING leader

HOW TO *develop* PEOPLE, *lead* TEAMS, AND *mentor* WELL

AUTHOR OF WOMEN AT WAR

JAN GREENWOOD

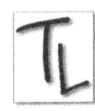

The Grace-Giving Leader. Copyright © 2020 by Jan Greenwood

All rights reserved. No portion of this publication may be reproduced, stored in a retrieval system, or transmitted in any form by any means—electronic, mechanical, photocopying, recording, or any other—except for brief quotations in printed reviews, without the prior permission of the publisher or author.

Published by Thrilling Life Publishers
P.O. Box 92522 | Southlake TX 76092 | www.thrillinglife.com

ISBN (print media): 978-0-9889240-3-1

Cover and Layout Design: Wendy K. Walters

Back Cover Image: Matthew Greenwood

Edited by: Victorya Rogers

Printed in the United States of America.

Unless otherwise noted at the Scripture reference, all verses within are taken from THE HOLY BIBLE, NEW INTERNATIONAL VERSION®, NIV® Copyright © 1973, 1978, 1984, 2011 by Biblica, Inc.™ Used by permission of Zondervan. All rights reserved worldwide.

Other versions contained within are as follows:

Scripture quotations marked NLT are taken from the HOLY BIBLE, NEW LIVING TRANSLATION, copyright © 1996, 2004, 2015 by Tyndale House Foundation. Used by permission of Tyndale House Publishers, a Division of Tyndale House Ministries, Carol Stream, Illinois 60188. All rights reserved.

Scriptures marked NKJV are taken from the NEW KING JAMES VERSION®. Copyright© 1982 by Thomas Nelson, Inc. Used by permission. All rights reserved.

Scriptures marked ESV are taken from the THE HOLY BIBLE, ENGLISH STANDARD VERSION® Copyright© 2001 by Crossway, a publishing ministry of Good News Publishers. Used by permission.

Scriptures marked AMP are taken from the AMPLIFIED® BIBLE, Copyright © 1954, 1958, 1962, 1964, 1965, 1987 by the Lockman Foundation Used by Permission. (www.Lockman.org)

Scripture marked MSG are taken from THE MESSAGE, copyright © 1993, 2002, 2018 by Eugene H. Peterson. Used by permission of NavPress. All rights reserved. Represented by Tyndale House Publishers, Inc.

Because of the dynamic nature of the Internet, any web addresses or links contained in this book may have changed since publication and may no longer be valid.

dedication

I dedicate this book to the many grace-giving leaders who have impacted my life. You have been often unnoticed, unseen or underestimated. Take heart. Your light shines bright in the souls of many spiritual children. You are a sharp arrow in the hand of the Master, a messenger of grace who changed my life.

acknowledgements

I have much gratitude in my heart when it comes to the making of this book. While it is certainly not the final authority on grace or leadership, I do believe it is a Spirit-inspired word that God has worked into my own life. Without the invitation of the Holy Spirit and the Word of God, this book would not exist. All the praise belongs to JESUS for His infinite love and sacrificial grace.

To my husband, MARK. Thank you for enduring this process with me and for believing in me enough to help push me across the finish line. I surely would have given up without your sacrifice and encouragement.

Thank you to GATEWAY CHURCH for investing in me for many years and for trusting me to lead. Thanks to the leadership, I have been mentored by some of the best Christian leaders in the world, and I am transformed as a result. Pastoring in this church has given me an opportunity to become a part of a family. For an only child, it's a big deal to feel like you have brothers and sisters—that you belong.

To the INCREDIBLE LEADERS who have gotten into the trenches with me to fight battles and to stay the course, thank you for being models of grace to me. Thank you to the entire GATEWAY CHURCH WOMEN'S MINISTRY TEAM that I worked directly with for years. So many of these lessons were learned alongside you. I am also grateful to the SOUTHLAKE CAMPUS LEADERSHIP, who have consistently encouraged me to share the message of my heart. And to my very own EQUIP TEAM that I minister with on a daily basis. Thank you for letting me practice what I am trying to preach. You are full of grace.

I am especially thankful for the people who have read, edited and responded to this content on multiple occasions. Thank you, KRISTIN LEMUS for being the spark that began it all. Thank you, WENDY K WALTERS, LORIANN BIGGERS, VICTORYA ROGERS, MARILYN and MIKE WEIHER, EMILY MILLER, CYNTHIA BAKER, and LORETTA MOERBE. Some of you gave me great ideas, some of you helped me craft the message for greater impact and clarity, and some of you held my feet to the fire believing I could do better.

I am honored by the contribution of the MANY WOMEN FEATURED IN THIS BOOK. You are a collective community of grace-giving leaders who have impacted my own leadership journey. You have chosen to share with vulnerability, transparency and authority. You gave this book fresh life and I am confident your testimony will mentor many.

Thank you to my publisher at Thrilling Life, VICTORYA ROGERS, for your friendship, your confidence and your hard work. This book became a reality because of your gifts and calling.

contents

FROM HOLLY WAGNER — 1
FOREWORD

THE JOURNEY OF GRACE — 3
INTRODUCTION

CHAPTER ONE — 15
LACED WITH GRACE

CHAPTER TWO — 33
GRACE TO WAIT

CHAPTER THREE — 69
THE POWER TO CHANGE

CHAPTER FOUR — 99
THE POWER TO INFLUENCE

CHAPTER FIVE — 129
THE POWER TO LEAD

CHAPTER SIX — 155
MAKE IT PERSONAL

REVIEW — 177
GRACE-GIVING LEADERSHIP SECRETS

APPENDIX — 179
ARE YOU A GRACE-GIVING LEADER?

GRACE-GIVING STUDY GUIDE — 183
DISCUSSION QUESTIONS FOR LEADERS

ABOUT THE AUTHOR — 195
MEET JAN GREENWOOD

from holly wagner

FOREWORD

For most of us taking a walk is easy. The challenge comes when we look behind and realize people are following. Over the past 25 years I have felt the responsibility to live my life in such a way that a younger woman could follow. The prophet Jeremiah challenges us to "mark our path."

> SET UP ROAD *signs;*
> PUT UP *guideposts.*
> MARK WELL THE *path*
> BY WHICH YOU CAME.
>
> JEREMIAH 31:21 NLT

How I handle challenge matters. Am I marking my trail with bitterness, frustration and envy or faith and hope? And how I handle favor is important. Am I putting up signposts of arrogance and entitlement or humility and service?

My friend Jan Greenwood has written a book that marks the trail of leadership with grace and strength. She is one of those women who have put up guideposts for others to follow. Over the last decade I have watched her lead teams and change environments with her strategy, her knowledge, her sense of fun and her gift of leadership. She has navigated challenge and favor and has done both with kindness and a determination to equip a younger generation.

She writes, "I think there are enough discrimination, roadblocks and hurdles for women along the way. We don't need to add to the difficulties by turning against one another. Rather we need to empower one another." In this book, this is exactly what she is doing. It is what she has done with her life. I love this woman and am honored to be on the leadership journey with her at this time in history.

Now is the time to become a woman that gives grace freely and, as a result, helps others rise up and follow.

HOLLY WAGNER
Co-Founding Pastor, Oasis Church, Los Angeles, CA
Founder, She Rises

The journey of grace

INTRODUCTION

My personal journey to becoming a grace-giving leader was long. I began by striving to earn each leadership position by proving myself every step of the way. I did not understand that when God calls you to lead others, He calls you by grace—not by works.

As an emerging leader without this understanding, I found myself wrestling with much uncertainty. Impatient to accomplish great things, I was often frustrated when obstacles were placed before me that seemed designed to hold me back. I was overly sensitive to other's opinions and strove to please everyone. I had an insatiable yearning to make a difference in the world by being part of something meaningful, but I knew nothing about the importance of grace as a powerful tool of leadership. Instead, I thought the answer was to ignore the discomfort in my heart and to just work harder.

That is why my husband called me "the Queen of de-Nile."

For years, I simply denied my feelings and just kept going. I wanted to prove myself to God and others. I did not want to stop and really look at the sensation of resistance that I later discovered was the presence of the Holy Spirit asking me to wait on His timing. I did not want to wait. After all, He created me competent with a willingness to help others. He put me in these leadership positions to do just that. So I pressed on adding even more projects and responsibilities in spite of my discomfort and impending burnout.

By ignoring that nudging on my heart, I soon began to believe I was entitled to more leadership positions. I thought, "They owed me." Somehow, someone was holding me back or even taking advantage of me. This kind of self-centered thinking led to many frustrating days of waiting on promotions that I believed were long past due. I didn't want to wait for what comes next. I was in a hurry. Surely God needed me to keep pushing forward so I could get all His work done.

During those early years, I would feel my head press against a leadership lid, a limitation or even a glass ceiling, and I would think, "Surely someone will see that I have earned advancement." When they didn't notice or seem to care, I just performed more. Blame would race along the edges of my mind and injustice would scream for relief. It became easy to believe I was personally rejected or disqualified and that someone or something was holding me back. Was it because I was a woman? I often felt overlooked, disqualified, unchosen, and left out. I struggled with thoughts like: "Maybe I'm not called," "God doesn't like me, trust me or care about my feelings." or "I must have missed it." There was also a struggle with hopelessness. I constantly battled the lies that my dreams will never come to pass and that I am doomed for failure and frustration.

My moment of truth came when I finally crashed, burned, and realized I was the one creating most of the proverbial glass ceilings all by myself. My need for recognition, acceptance, and success was creating a leadership lid on my life. I couldn't be trusted by God to lead sooner or greater, because my own heart was not at peace. In His unsurpassed wisdom, God frustrated my plans and resisted my strategies in order to sift out my selfishness and insecurity. If I had advanced easily, according to my own plan of action, I would have spent my whole life trying to work to earn what God wanted to give me for free.

It's called grace.

Every time I strove for recognition, He comforted me with His presence. Every time I wondered if my gender was the problem, He accepted me. Every time I wanted to shatter the hindrances and obstacles I perceived, He gave me the grace to wait. I'm so glad I did. I have learned priceless lessons over these years and I want to give these insights to you, dear friend. I want to encourage you to become a grace-giving leader through the pages of this book.

If you are concerned about the glass ceilings in your own life, I assure you that they are more effectively and more quickly shattered by grace than by hammers. I also assure you that all of us have a glass ceiling formed by grace. It protects us from our own foolishness. It guards and shepherds our future and prepares us with a greater capacity to love.

> GRACE *shatters* GLASS CEILINGS MORE EFFECTIVELY AND MORE QUCKLY THAN *hammers*

While I spent a lot of time over the years lost in performance and striving to do it all on my own, I knew I needed help. I really longed for a mentor. I wanted someone who would actually see me and support me. It took me a long time to realize that mentors were already all around me. They just didn't look like what I was searching for or what I thought I needed in the moment. As a result, I often walked alone. I was blind to the resources and support that were already available.

This idea that I could change the way I view myself and others through a lens of grace instead of a lens of performance began as a seed of hope in my heart. That hope eventually broke through my hard shell of self-protection opening my eyes to the continuing patterns of self-sabotage that limited my leadership.

That season of growth and maturity eventually led to a greater intention on my part to learn from others, embrace my passion to lead, and allow God to stretch my understanding of what it means to do those things with grace.

It's taken me five years to write this book. The original draft came easily. I was at a critical moment in my own health journey, and I was experiencing tremendous grace. People were loving me well, and in spite of the threat of the moment, I was being carried on the wings of prayer. I was at peace in the midst of war. I was on a temporary leave from work, and found myself with a lot of time in mandatory rest. There were not enough outlets to share my journey or to express my gratitude. The work had been stirring in me for about two years, and I had already taught on the very basic principles you will find here. I started playing with an idea, and then I found that something very special began to flow from deep within.

Transformation is powerful like that. When you can tap the place in your heart, and for a moment, find an expression that captures it, you can overflow with love and grace. I unintentionally came out of that crisis moment with a new message and a greater sense of hope. Over the past five years, the waiting has tested the message. I've grown and understood so much more. As a result, what you hold in your hands is some of the best wine of my life—aged and seasoned by grace. I am so humbled and honored to get to share these lessons with you.

As I am drafting the final edits to this book, we are in the midst of a worldwide pandemic. Our culture is in shock, and our nation is in turmoil. Every single person around the world has been touched. If ever we needed a vision for healthy leadership, it is now.

Maybe that's why this project is coming to fruition in this moment. You and I are intersecting at a critical moment in God's plan to make Himself known to all, and you have a part to play. Every believer must become a leader. Your faith journey is on display, and those who are within your sphere need the grace you carry within. That is why this book is so timely. I don't want this generation of influencers to struggle as hard and as long as I did to understand the power of grace and its impact on your leadership life.

Who you choose to do life with either expands your dreams or limits your boundaries. I want your dreams to be expanded. I want you to find trusted counsel and practical resources to build wisdom and understanding that can change your life. I highly recommend finding a mentor as one of the people in your circle of friends. Mentoring is a pure form of discipleship. It is time-proven and incredibly impactful. A genuine relationship with a seasoned mentor is an invaluable asset to anyone who aspires to intentionally influence others.

My own life has been transformed by the influence of many mentoring relationships. Some I knew personally—some are even relatives. Others I found in the pages of Scripture or the pleasure of an autobiography. Sometimes I rubbed shoulders with a wiser woman at a critical life stage, and often I watched, gleaned, and learned from afar. When I encountered Jesus Christ, I began the most loving and empowering relationship I have ever known. His love for people and my value for relationships lit a life-long passion in me to build up and encourage others.

Through the pages of this book I want to be part of your journey and mentor you. Please allow this to be my investment in you and your leadership just as others invested in me.

Why should you follow me? Why should you trust my counsel?

For more than thirty years, I've been studying leaders. One of my most significant leadership roles began when I became a mom of four kids. I also worked outside my home and served as a leader in my local church. I held leadership positions in the marketplace and within the business my husband and I owned. I have been a fund-raising consultant for several Christian ministries and have even run a non-profit educational organization. I eventually established a ministry called Brave Strong Girl and wrote a book about healthy female relationships called *Women at War: Declaring A Cease-Fire On Toxic Female Relationships*.

For more than a decade I have been serving as a part of the pastoral team at Gateway Church in the Dallas/Fort Worth Metroplex. For about eight years I helped to lead a team and direct a beautiful conference for women called Pink Impact. It was a transformational experience to serve alongside our senior pastor's wife and women's ministry leader, Pastor Debbie Morris. Currently, I serve as the Pastor of Equip at our

Southlake campus where one of my most important responsibilities is to disciple, engage and mentor the next generation of leaders.

I have been discipled by some of the most influential Christian leaders of our day, and I have been inspired as well by a community of leaders who are both friends and family to me. I am so excited to introduce you to many of them throughout this book. Not only will I feature in each chapter a particularly impactful grace-giving leader in my own life, but I will also be sharing the experience and the advice of a variety of leaders who are worthy of your following. I encourage you to take the time to get to know them more. Each one has so much to offer to you.

Of course I'm going to be sharing with you about my own journey. I know you will relate to my pain and failures, but I want you to also relate to my healing. Because of God's grace and the intersection of my life with grace-giving leaders, I have laid down the leadership tools of control and management to pick up the power of love and grace.

I've discovered a few principles that came to me like secrets on this journey. Mysteries that were revealed became principles upon which I lead and mentor today. These secrets truly work. They are secrets that empower rather than discourage, that ignite passion rather than destroy dreams, and that create successful teams rather than lone rangers.

I want to share these secrets with you.

Just to be clear, this book isn't going to tell you about how to increase your social media presence, sell more widgets, or build a personal empire. You can find that information elsewhere.

Instead, I am urging you to step out and bravely explore what it means to lead yourself and others from a place of grace. I am challenging you to push past self-doubt and interrupt your fears with courage. You will encounter the truth that the highest levels of leadership have very little to do with position, title or public accolades. They have lots to do with learning to create safe, confident, empowering environments where everyone gets to become their best.

HOW TO USE THIS INTERACTIVE BOOK

I don't want this to be just another book on leadership. My hope is that you will experience this book. My desire is that as you gain knowledge and understanding you will not just store it away like a book on a shelf. Rather, I encourage you to bring your discoveries to the table of life and learn to apply the principles within.

This book includes ten secrets included in chapters 2 through 5. Each secret ends with questions designed for your personal reflection. I have called these sections Pause and Ponder. In addition, I have included an addendum with ten questions for each of the six chapters for group discussion or personal study. You can take all the questions throughout the book to a whole new level of impact by discussing them with others, and as a group, submitting your ideas to one another and the Holy Spirit.

These prompts are not meant for a mental or intellectual process only. Rather I want you to learn to think, listen and ponder with others. Thinking about a question all by yourself limits you to your own experience, beliefs and current leadership lid. Don't rush pass these opportunities. Slow down. Listen. Think. Discuss. This simple practice will improve your leadership skills exponentially. More importantly, you will be developing a habit that every leader desperately needs of asking a great question, followed by quieting yourself enough to listen and think before you speak. This is a habit that every leader desperately needs. Of course inviting the Holy Spirit into your thought process helps you open up your inner man to perspectives and answers you can't find alone. It is possible to be discipled in a topic without being discipled in the Spirit.

So how do you ponder and process with God? Just begin by quieting your own thoughts. Maybe spend a few moments in prayer or worship. Then position yourself to listen. Ask the Holy Spirit a question and wait. Consider journaling your thoughts. Then ask yourself if what you are sensing and thinking lines up with the written Word of God. The Scripture is the final authority in testing all claims about what is true and right.

> ALL SCRIPTURE IS *given* BY INSPIRATION OF GOD, AND IS PROFITABLE FOR DOCTRINE, FOR REPROOF, FOR CORRECTION, FOR INSTRUCTION IN RIGHTEOUSNESS, THAT THE MAN OF GOD MAY BE *complete,* THOROUGHLY *equipped* FOR EVERY GOOD WORK.
>
> 2 TIMOTHY 3:16-17 NKJV

> CALL TO ME, AND I WILL *answer* YOU, AND *show* YOU *great* AND *mighty* THINGS, WHICH YOU DO NOT KNOW.
>
> JEREMIAH 33:3 NKJV

> I WILL *instruct* YOU
> AND *teach* YOU IN THE WAY
> YOU SHOULD GO;
> I WILL *guide* YOU WITH MY EYE.
>
> PSALM 32:8 NKJV

> BUT THE *helper*, THE HOLY SPIRIT, WHOM THE FATHER WILL *send* IN MY NAME, HE WILL *teach* YOU ALL THINGS, AND *bring* TO YOUR REMEMBRANCE ALL THINGS THAT I *said* TO YOU.
>
> JOHN 14:26 NKJV

The pattern of seeking to connect with God and to understand His counsel through the Bible is a self-leadership skill that is priceless. Of all creation, only mankind was created with the ability to reflect, evaluate and intentionally change our minds. This advantage, well developed and deeply loved, will lead you toward a life that is sincerely satisfying and full of purpose.

The journey of becoming a grace-giving leader will neither be easy nor painless. In fact, it's going to be costly. It will require you to be vulnerable, authentic and transparent. You may feel exposed and afraid. You will need wisdom, practical advice and input from other people for real connection. Most of all, you will need the Word of God and the Holy Spirit's divine power and inspiration.

I'm eager to intersect your life in this critical season of your development as a leader. Whether you are a young woman embarking on your first leadership assignment, a more experienced woman in a season of transition, or one who is aiming high in the workforce or nonprofit sector, this book is for you. Together, we will launch out on a journey of personal growth and leadership development so that you can help as many other people as possible.

If your heart is set on a journey to serve, love, and lead, then you'll live a life that is rich, full, and gratifying. More importantly, your life will grasp the real and ultimate mission of every leader—to train others in this way of life.

Today, I challenge you to accept God's commission and to go far and near in grace. God authorized and commanded me to commission you:

> GO out AND train EVERYONE YOU MEET, far AND near, IN THIS WAY OF LIFE".
>
> MATTHEW 28:18 MSG

God's protection over you
Guarded with truth
Generously given Glorify Him
Receive salvation
Releasing Christ's power within
Righteousness of God
Acquitted & justified by Jesus
Always loved A heart for others
Accomplishing God's purpose
Cherished Compassionate
Complete restoration
Come as you are
Christ ahead of you
Every burden lifted & battle won
Empowered by the Holy Spirit
Endless love of God Expectant
PS. Rom 5:8

@prayerfulsigns

CREATED BY AMBER COLBERG, CEO OF PRAYERFUL SIGNS, LLC

chapter one

LACED WITH GRACE

Years ago, my husband and I moved from a small town in Arkansas to west Texas to attend a local university. We were so excited when, right out of college, Mark was accepted into a management program with a Fortune 500 retailer. His career was taking off as he was promoted every year or so. With each promotion, we moved, and I found myself in search of a new job. I had done a variety of work, but nothing that I thought was cool or exciting.

Then I landed the dream job.

I went to work as an assistant to an executive in a small consulting firm that served several large non-profit Christian organizations around the nation. She was smart, polished and had been in the field of advertising for years. She was "up and coming" bringing to the company a passion and experience level that was opening more doors and producing new customers. She was powerful, a decision maker and a woman who knew how to lead. I attached my dreams to her coattails of success and wanted to be just like her.

I helped my boss establish an office in a beautiful high-rise building. We bought expensive furniture and stocked the kitchen with free drinks and snacks. Every day I wore a suit (a big deal to me in the 80's). I unlocked the office and managed her clients and office work while she traveled all over the United States. We got along well, and I did a good job of assisting her. My skills were soon recognized in our other offices and I was promoted to a junior consultant. I began to earn my keep by learning to develop billable hours for a portion of my time.

When I was invited to travel a bit and support another consultant on the team, things started to shift. I soon found that the more others wanted my help, the more critical she became of my work. I responded by ramping up my efforts, determined to please her and prove my worth. I tried harder and harder, but things got more and more tense. I couldn't put my finger on the problem, but I knew one of us had shifted.

Then one day, I made a huge mistake. I faxed (don't laugh – it was the latest in high tech communication) a private piece of correspondence to the wrong client. That client was a competitor of another one of our clients.

Within an hour, I got a phone call from my boss asking questions that were difficult. My mistake was revealed, and I was duly embarrassed. I apologized fervently, but I did not realize how significant my error was until the president of the company called me from the home office to let me know the ramifications.

Although I didn't lose my job that day, I did lose the support of my boss. She no longer trusted me, and within a short amount of time, I didn't trust her either. She bore the embarrassment and consequences with the clients. As a result, she ultimately lost faith in me. I felt so ashamed and unsafe that within about six weeks I chose to quit the dream job. I left the company humiliated and burned. I blamed her. Thirty years later I can assure you it was not her fault, but I can also tell you she extended me no grace.

In my anger, I declared I would never make such a stupid mistake again. This became an impossible inner vow to keep. It led to many disappointments over the years because, of course, I made many more mistakes.

Sometimes I look back on that moment and I still feel the sting of embarrassment and my sadness at the loss of the job. However, what actually stuck with me for years were the inner vows I had made: "It's not okay to make mistakes;" "Don't count on others when the going gets rough;" and "Don't trust women." These lies, along with my already firmly rooted people pleasing patterns set me steadfastly on a path of self-sufficiency and fear of people.

Over the years I became just like that executive woman who had been my boss. I led well but withheld full trust and support. If someone began to excel, I would feel threatened. If they made a major mistake, I took responsibility, tried to correct it and harbored resentment toward them. I simply did not extend grace to others or to myself. I was harsh in my judgments and foolish in my thinking.

Looking back, I now realize that I thought my former boss owed me something more. I had worked hard to prove myself worthy, and I didn't think one mistake should be so costly. I did not understand that people do not owe me anything. If you work and get a paycheck, it's called a wage. That is all that is owed to you. Loyalty, favor, patience or even a promotion are not something to be expected or demanded. By their very nature they can only be given to you as gifts of grace.

I wonder what giving and receiving grace would have looked like in that situation. It certainly wouldn't have meant that there were not consequences, for I surely needed accountability, additional training, closer supervision or even a period of probation. But what if that process had bent me toward an experience of grace? What if I had been forgiven? What if I had been given a chance to apologize to our customer? What if I had been coached in moving forward? What if I had survived it?

It's probably no surprise to you that people do not flourish in harsh, frightening or abusive situations. They don't respond well to know-it-alls or bullies. They leave leaders and organizations who are selfish, and they crumble under constant criticism and ungracious treatment.

> PEOPLE DO NOT *flourish* IN HARSH, FRIGHTENING, OR ABUSIVE *situations*

On the other hand, people do grow in safe, kind and encouraging environments. They thrive when treated with graceful words or deeds. They flourish alongside a forerunner who speaks with wisdom and leads with grace.

If you have experienced significant kindness or nurture, your personal leadership bent will be toward giving grace to others. If you have experienced pain, failure or even rejection at the hands of a leader or a lover, your bent will lean toward rules, regulations, control and management.

No matter what your bent, I want to help bend you toward Christ and His example so that you can see and experience everything in your life through the lens of grace. Why grace? Because I believe that grace is a powerful gift from God. Grace arrives in our lives in the form of strength or courage or kindness or care. It is the doorway to salvation and the road upon which our discipleship journey is laid. Yes, it is undeserved favor—a free gift to every believer in Jesus Christ. But more than that, grace is power. It is a divine enablement that produces an anointing in your life. It makes you powerful when you are weak and able to heal when you've been wounded. It makes you influential in the lives of others. It empowers you to lead people with the grace you've been given.

What comes to mind when you think of being a leader? Do you imagine yourself as the captain of your own fate? Do you see yourself standing in front of others, giving a charge? Or maybe you imagine yourself hiding on the back row, looking at your feet and hoping no one calls your name. Some of us are eager to be handed the reigns of leadership while others fear the responsibility. Both of those perspectives are extremes.

I am one of those eager for the reigns. I have always dreamed of leading. I can't quite explain it. Since I was a little girl, I have had confidence in myself that I would know what to do in a situation if people would just listen and obey. As you can imagine, my leadership journey has had a few bumps and bruises along the way due to such a prideful heart. Over the years, I have had to evaluate why I want to lead and consider how I can do it more effectively.

A part of that process has been my discovery and following of some mentors who have substantially impacted my thinking, experience and expression of leadership. God has been so faithful to introduce me to these leaders at critical moments in my journey. With the advantage of hindsight, I can see how God brings people into our lives who are meant to impart gifts, share vision and challenge us to be brave.

In the very early days of my call to serve as a women's leader in my local church, I came across a unique voice that seemed to understand the secret desires, concerns and weaknesses of my heart. Holly Wagner was an emerging force among Christian women leaders. She was already known for her leadership within Oasis Church, a diverse and thriving Christian community in the heart of Los Angeles that she co-founded and co-pastored with her husband, Phillip. She also had a recognized and growing ministry to women called God Chicks. Today Holly is a prolific author having written many books. She preaches at conferences around the world and ministers to her community of women called She Rises. I don't remember how I first became aware of Holly, but I can remember with great clarity how her life and message impacted my journey.

When I read Holly's book, *God Chicks: Living Life as a 21st Century Woman*, I knew I had found someone who "got me." In my tiny little church in Abilene, Texas I often felt so strange and insecure. I had big passion and big dreams. In fact, they were so big that I was a little ashamed of my zeal and very intimidated by the concern that I might violate a spiritual boundary of leadership just because of my gender. Holly was powerful and deeply rooted in the Word of God. She was confident, but not arrogant. Beautiful, but not prissy. Empowering, but never condescending. I wanted to know so much more.

Holly mentored me for years from a distance, completely unaware of my existence. Both her teaching and her writing influenced me. I embraced the wisdom found in her books entitled: *Warrior Chicks: Rising Strong When Life Wants to Take You Down; Love Works: Develop Healthy*

Relationships in a "Love Broken" World; and her most recent release, *Find Your Brave: Courage to Stand Strong When the Waves Crash In.* These messages changed my perspective and grew my Biblical foundation for service and leadership. She made me feel like I was a part of this community of women and that God found me trustworthy. I began to grow in confidence and in calling.

It was in this transition from a small beginning that I could see how God used my season there to prepare me for the greater responsibility to come. It is so important to not despise those small beginnings and to trust God as you grow in your leadership. Trusting Him to use every bit of everything He instills in you is part of what makes this faith-filled life so incredible.

It was during the course of this growth, that I transitioned from serving as a volunteer lay women's pastor in a congregation of about 250 people in West Texas to supernaturally becoming a part of the women's ministry team in a congregation of about 6,000 members at that time. In joining Gateway Church, located in the Dallas/Fort Worth area, I found myself right in the center of a community of women who were in love with Jesus, empowered to minister and full of huge vision. My heart was on fire, and I knew I had found a home. A church. A community where I could connect and grow.

While my responsibilities and influence were small, I was invited to contribute to the work of the ministry. As I served, I naturally became a

> **TRUSTING GOD TO** *use* **EVERY BIT OF** *everything* **HE INSTILLS IN YOU IS PART OF WHAT** *makes* **THIS FAITH-FILLED LIFE SO** *incredible*

part of the team who worked on Gateway's women's conference entitled Pink Impact. As a result, I was introduced to other influential female voices including Christine Caine, Priscilla Shirer, Charlotte Gambill, Lisa Bevere and so many more. It would be a few years, but eventually Holly Wagner was invited to the Pink Impact platform.

When I finally met Holly, I remember being attracted to her lack of insecurity, her ability to preach and to teach. Most of all, it was her passion to raise up other women leaders, especially those who were called to pastor within churches and para ministries. I also remember that, although my position was insignificant, Holly took the time to connect with me. She didn't say or do anything extraordinary. She simply honored me with her friendship.

I didn't just want you to know Holly through my eyes. I wanted you to hear from her directly. So I asked her to share her heart on grace-giving leadership.

HOLLY WAGNER

Leadership is something that has always been a part of my personality from childhood. I was always that child who got people to follow me. That doesn't always mean I led others the right way. In fact, I think it led a few right into trouble! But things seemed to work themselves out as I got older and I took on leadership of youth groups in high school.

After moving to California, I met my Phillip. We fell in love and married. At the time, I was acting, and he was in ministry. Being honest, I wasn't sure what leadership in ministry looked like. It started with serving in the church and helping where it was needed, but with my leadership gifting it soon turned into leading a team of greeters, or people in children's ministry. Whatever door opened, wherever the need was, I served.

Great leadership includes grace. As a leader, I needed to extend grace to people no matter where they were in their own journey. I needed to recognize that others had the potential to lead and should be leading. For me, leadership happened in what seemed to be a very natural progression, but that's not the case for everyone.

After reading Titus chapter two this one time, it jumped off the page at me that I had a responsibility as an older woman to bring in the next generation. Ministry at the time though seemed to be heavier, spiritually speaking, and we were losing the younger generation. I needed to change the way I communicated. I wanted to teach truth and have Holy Spirit moments, but also have fun! And that became the model for God Chicks which has now become She Rises.

It started as a quarterly gathering at my church, and then it grew to a conference for women from all over. I felt such a responsibility for these women, but especially for the 20 women pastors who had come to that first conference. Spontaneously, I asked them all to lunch which we had in our nursery because it was the only room with chairs! And that was the beginning of She Leads. It was the moment I realized I could help speak into leaders.

As I taught these leaders, I wanted to affirm women pastors that this was not about having conferences. Leading women was about reaching others, lifting them up and inspiring them. It's about extending grace and leading from right where you are. It's about sharing the pitfalls of comparison and affirming women in their own gifts and talents to give to others what they have. It's passing the baton and realizing that every leader has their part to fulfill and not being afraid to let go and release them to begin leading others also.

Grace-filled leadership is remembering that this leadership journey is about fruitfulness. It's about the parable of the talents and growing what's been given to us, what's in our hand. And as we grow what's in our hand, we can help others grow what's in theirs.

Holly has mentored me through all kinds of seasons and challenges, and most of the time, she was probably unaware I was following her. She is a breast cancer survivor. She was one of the first women to reach out to me when she heard about my diagnosis, and she has shown me how to walk well in the face of adversity. I have learned to keep my focus and leadership on God's promises and not my weakness. That is why I reached out and asked her to write the foreword of this book. She is a forerunner of graceful leadership, and her endorsement means so much to me.

What drew me to Holly was that, like me, she too was always eager to be a leader. But not all leaders are like Holly and me. Some leaders are more like Esther—reluctant to lead but obedient when called to do so. What I discovered as I began working under the leadership and discipleship of Pastor Debbie Morris, was how much I could learn from a woman who described herself as a reluctant leader.

Pastor Debbie is a dear friend and precious gift to me. Our journey began in the midst of a tumultuous season of transition for her at Gateway Church. I had been hired by an interim leader, and when

Debbie returned to the leadership position, she really had no reason to keep me on her team. Not only did she not know me, but I was radically different and immature in my spiritual journey. It was a mircle of grace that she gave me a chance to grow and learn while serving with her. She trusted me when she had no evidence that I was trustworthy. She immediately began to lead me toward a kinder, more tender and grace-filled expression of leadership.

I can share with you that the first person who taught me about grace or being a grace-giving leader is Pastor Debbie Morris. I still have my notes from a message she taught entitled "Leading With Grace." She defined leadership as a responsibility of stewardship and a requirement to be faithful with whatever influence God gives to you. This thrust toward Christlikeness was inspiring to me. Despite the tremendous influence that she carries, she is a servant rather than a celebrity. She lives a life of self-sacrifice and love for others. So many times, I watched her trust God with impossible circumstances, challenges and people. She has always been devoted to unity and generously shares with others the blessing that comes as a result. If Pastor Robert Morris' life message is generosity, I like to think Pastor Debbie's message is grace.

I had the great privilege of working directly with Debbie for about eight years. I never found her to deviate from this pattern of leadership. Debbie had quite a challenge in leading me. I needed to be seeded with humility, patience and trust. She had to uproot insecurity and mistrust within me. She taught me how to care about people over projects and how to trust leadership even when I didn't understand a decision or a boundary. And when the time came for me to transition to a new responsibility, she blessed me, released me, and sent me out with both gifts and grace. She is still my pastor today, and I am humbled to be her friend and follower.

One of the highlights of my years with Pastor Debbie was during the season she was writing her book, *The Blessed Woman: Learning About Grace from the Women of the Bible*. Not only did I learn so much more about her journey, but also I gained an understanding of the importance of the women of the Bible. I discovered that Esther, Mary, Hannah, Miriam, Deborah and Naomi should and could be mentors and guides for my own journey. If you want to know the heart of this gentle leader, you will find it on the pages of her book.

Although Pastor Debbie might not choose the public leadership responsibilities she holds, her impact is huge because she trusts God more than herself and embraces whatever assignment she is given with wisdom, love and grace. She understands what it took me years to grasp which is that leaders are servants—not bosses.

I'm not the only one who has been impacted by grace-giving leaders like Pastor Debbie and Holly Wagner. My friend, Amber Colberg, has become a grace-giving leader by embracing her personal passion to help others align with God's purpose for them and their life. Using her prophetic gifts, she founded an online business named Prayerful Signs where she designs a line of custom products that utilize acrostic poetry and prayer to speak truth and encouragement into the hearts of others. You might have noticed her work at the end of the Introduction, where I shared her inspirational acrostic design for "grace." Here's what Amber has to say about her experience with grace-giving leaders.

> I remember the grace-giving leaders that God lovingly placed in my life on more than one occasion. In a season when I felt overwhelmed by hardship and pain, I found myself searching for God's outstretched hand to carry me through. I was so

> uncertain, and I had so many questions. The grace-giving leaders in my life recognized my pain, prayed with me and for me, encouraged me in my position in Christ, and offered tangible grace to me. Being a grace-giving leader goes beyond what we can see. For me, it was about the leaders extending that outstretched hand I was searching for, and I experienced the immense love and grace of God through them.

I love that Amber was propelled forward through a difficult transition by reaching out and trusting other leaders to speak into her life. Today she passes that blessing along. But you don't need to start a business or a ministry to demonstrate grace-giving leadership.

Next, please notice how new mom and friend, Jacquelyn Beckworth, shares how she intentionally invites others into her world to connect and disciple them.

> I try to be available. In this season of life, I'm a first-time momma and my time and energy pretty much all go into my family. I still try to make myself available. I invite girls over to our house and chat with them on the couch while Liam plays on the floor. My husband and I look at the calendar for the week and intentionally set aside discipleship time for both of us to invest in others. Whatever season I'm in, I try to be available and welcome others in.
>
> There are two female pastors that I have worked with who have had the most influence in my leadership journey. These women invited me into their lives. This was huge for me. I've heard it said before that mentorship says, 'take me to coffee' while discipleship says, 'take me with you.' Because they

opened their lives to me, I have been deeply discipled. I am so grateful.

Jacquelyn reminds me that we can be grace-giving in every season of our life. Ever since I've known her, she's had a heart to encourage other young women.

Rhonda Love is a new friend from the past few years whom I divinely connected with when we crossed paths. She just retired from 40 years in human resources, and served 14 years on staff at her local church. Rhonda's presence is powerful, bringing peace and confidence into every conversation. She's also passionate about discipleship and prayer. Even though she's retired, she's not finished. As she looks forward to the next season of leadership, I asked her to share about who mentored her.

> It began when I signed up to volunteer as an altar worker at church. Although I knew I had the desire and passion to pray for others, the group leader saw something more in me that I had no idea was there. I knew nothing about effective intercessory prayer. She took me under her wing, led me to the Bible, taught me how to study the word of God, and how to pray His Word over others. She poured herself into me even investing resources—a Bible and a devotional to help me become consistent. Sitting with her, opening the Word and praying together changed my life. Today, I still have both books and refer to them often.
>
> As she began to have some health challenges, she asked me to take over the Sunday morning prayer team. I was shocked. There were others I felt were more qualified, but she said, "God qualifies the called." And she was sure I was ready! As

one of her sweetest gifts to me and one of her last prayer assignments, she met with our women's ministry pastor. They invited me to take over her position as Prayer Team Leader for all of our women's events and conferences. This woman, led by grace, prepared me for one of the most important responsibilities of my life. She showed me how to live with Jesus at my center and how to always point others to Him and His Word.

Sometimes grace-giving includes correction, redirection and greater discipleship. Kerrie Oles was able to humbly receive counsel and change course because she and her mentor have a deep and abiding relationship. Kerrie is an author, inspirational Bible teacher and founder of Unlocked Ministries and *The Best You* podcast. She passionately serves as an evangelist and teacher to a growing community of women who have experienced significant pain or trauma in their lives leading them to health and wholeness. We've spiritually grown up together, having started out in ministry around the same time, and we have encouraged one another all along the way. Kerrie recently shared the following with me:

> I remember thinking that our ministry was ready for an "office space," so we went forward with a plan and signed a one-year lease. I never asked my mentor for her advice in advance, but when we entered a financially challenging season, I went to her for counsel. When she found out we were struggling, she confidently and with such grace said, "I feel like your office space is draining important funds that could be put to better use."
>
> I resisted her counsel because I didn't want to relinquish the space. I felt like it made us seem more of a legitimate

functioning ministry. She waited until we were together in private to ask me about the reasons I desired the office space. That day she was able to help me see that if the ministry was designed to really help and heal others, then the public's perceptions were not something I should be concerned with. We gave up the office space shortly after that. It was the best decision. Otherwise I feel sure we would have had to close the ministry. By doing so, our ministry began to thrive because we were able to give more to people. By listening to loving correction from my mentor, something that could have been a stumbling block for our future was privately and graciously addressed.

With all that's going on in the world today, I continue to be so thankful for her guidance. Because of her grace-filled counsel, I now look through the same lens as "the office space" experience with every decision I make. I now seek counsel, consider my options and pray. I've become a much wiser decision maker and a better leader.

The investment you make in others and the wisdom you share can not only propel someone along in their journey, but can also rescue them from danger, missteps or threats while equipping them to become more effective leaders.

Whether you are the "raise your hand first" person or the "oh no, not me" person, you are needed as a leader. Whether you feel weak or strong, courageous or fearful, certain or insecure, God can and will invite you into relationships that are ripe for His grace. God has spotted you and he is undeterred by your concerns. He's called you out. You can trust God. Even when man fails, God will not. Remember this verse:

> BUT HE SAID TO ME, "MY *grace* IS *sufficient* FOR YOU, FOR MY *power* IS MADE *perfect* IN *weakness*." THEREFORE, I WILL BOAST ALL THE MORE *gladly* ABOUT MY WEAKNESSES, SO THAT CHRIST'S *power* MAY *rest* ON ME.
>
> 2 CORINTHIANS 12:9

GRACE (n):

THE *exercise* OF LOVE,
KINDNESS, MERCY, FAVOR;
A DISPOSITION TO *benefit*
OR *serve* ANOTHER.

chapter two

GRACE TO WAIT

A large part of my leadership journey began in the waiting. There were the years before my salvation—a long season of self-sufficiency and exhaustion—where I danced around the edges of religion and tried to be a good girl. Salvation finally pushed me past that point, but then a second season of waiting began. When I was finally surrendered to Christ, the Holy Spirit began a two-part work in my character.

First of all, I experienced a sense of destiny; I believed that I had a greater purpose and that my life mattered. Over the years, I came to understand my personal calling and my gifts. The result was a dream in my heart to lead and influence many for the glory of God.

Secondly, the presence of God in me began to expose the deficiency of my character. Rather than setting me out in a leadership role I thought I was ready to handle, the Holy Spirit started to slow me down. I began the essential work of waiting on God for the grace to grow and change.

God creates seasons of service, obscurity, or waiting so that we might turn to Him for our validation and our assignment. In effect, God is doing what He is asking you to do. He is waiting. He is waiting to privately highlight and transform the parts of you that need to be altered, healed or changed. We extend the season of waiting because we are stubborn, often refusing the private instruction, correction or discipline of the Holy Spirit. If we refuse to do the work because we fear the pain or despise the discomfort, we simply delay what must be accomplished. In fact, we hinder the work of the Holy Spirit in our lives.

No one escapes the call to wait. Just consider the people of the Bible. David was anointed king of Israel at 17. He was appointed king of Judah at 30 and over all of Israel at 33. Paul encountered Christ on the road to Damascus. He was appointed as an apostle 13 years later. Moses knew he was called at 40 but he was anointed at the burning bush to lead the people out of captivity at the age of 80. Even Jesus knew he was anointed at 12, but he was appointed at 30 to reveal Himself and His work to others.

Waiting upon God's grace equals preparation. Preparation is essential if you want to be a leader that others want to follow. Only fools rush into challenges with the wrong equipment, limited resources or sheer ignorance. The wise take the time to do the work necessary to develop their character and their skills. If you will wait patiently while investing in your own development, you will be able to face every upcoming challenge with confidence and grace.

In my experience, waiting is harder than doing, especially if you have a burning in your heart to make God famous. No one struggles more with the waiting than the girl who is prone to the doing. I'm a doer. Maybe that's why I fell in love with Katie Reid so easily; she's a doer too.

Katie and I first crossed paths through a mutual friend. We were participating in a conference for Christian women communicators. I had just recently released my book, *Women at War*, and another friend, Kristin Lemus, had been graciously sharing it with her friends. Katie was one of the first adopters. She was so gracious when we met, encouraging me on my own journey of publishing.

Katie has the ability to cut to the chase about matters of the heart while creating an environment of safety and love. She calls herself a "modern Martha" and helps so many of us who can relate. She encourages us to exchange our try-hard striving for hope-filled freedom as we settle into our position as a doer and a daughter.

It wouldn't be long until Katie would release her book, *Made Like Martha: Good News for the Woman Who Gets Things Done*. She is impacting so many lives by helping overachievers discover what it means to rest as God's daughter without compromising their God-given design as a doer. She helped me recalibrate and find strength in service and peace, even when I was tested and weak.

Katie is a spiritual mom and mentor to many. She first serves her own five kids then the Central Church community in central Michigan where her husband, Adam, serves as the pastor. Katie also serves a broader scope of women through her podcast, *The Martha and Mary Show*, in addition to books, songs and teaching. Long before I met her, she was encouraging others to walk out the wisdom found in God's Word. It makes sense to me that she relates more to Martha in Luke 10 than Martha's sister Mary. She's always checking off an item on her to-do list, and, by her own confession, she prefers to work rather than relax.

If you have a secret sympathy for Martha, you are going to love meeting my friend, Katie Reid.

KATIE REID

I have always been a doer—a planner who gets things done. My dad says that I've also always been a leader, even from the hospital nursery. According to him, I let out a wail and the rest followed suit. But even as someone born to lead, I have had a lot of learning and growing to do.

Over the years, I've matured into the leadership I now have. I have taken the time to observe both positive and negative examples of leadership and glean from them the necessary tools I needed to be a grace-based leader. The biggest turning point for me was moving away from a lifestyle of legalism. I had to step into the wide-open field of grace.

It was in taking that step that God revealed to me that I was already loved by Him. I didn't have to "do" anything to earn it. And, just like His love, I had to learn His grace was also a gift to be received and not a prize to be earned. I had to come to understand that although I was made like Martha to be a doer, I could also sit like Mary and just be a receiver.

In this understanding, I was free to lead from a place of being settled. I was free to sit down spiritually and exchange my try-hard striving for hope-filled freedom without abandoning how I was made. I was able to exchange the panic of the constant and sometimes over-doing for His peace. I had to stop micromanaging myself and others. I had to walk in the freedom that comes from realizing things were not all up to me.

God in His graciousness affirmed me in my innate design as a doer. He didn't condemn me for liking to check things off of my to-do list. But He did have to remind me that my worth did not come from those check marks.

I felt led to extend this same grace to other women who were walking out their design to be doers. I wanted other women who were like Martha to understand they didn't have to change and become Mary to be accepted. In writing *Made Like Martha: Good News for the Woman Who Gets Things Done*, my hope is that other doers love themselves as they are made and learn to find the balance between doing and sitting, between Martha and Mary.

Having grown into a grace-based leader, I invite others to find their footing in a life-giving environment where they feel valued and trusted. I encourage others to walk in freedom and live out their unique God-given purpose with grace and intention. I am intentional about being led by grace-based leaders like Jan so that I can then lead others by and with grace to be who they are, as God designed them, Martha or Mary.

Recently I was speaking with Katie, and she shared some insights about how to be a great grace-giving leader. They are worth sharing with you.

> Realize that there are many different personalities, perspectives, and approaches. Not everyone thinks like you or sees things in the same way. Learn to value the insights of others and ask God to help you see things from other people's

perspectives. Empathy and compassion are so important when it comes to loving and leading others. When someone feels heard, seen, valued, and understood, they will be more inclined to rise to the occasion and give their best.

Even in the midst of a full life, we can rest within, because of what Christ has done for us. Through our belief in Jesus' finished work on the cross, we are freed from trying to earn that which has already been given to us as a gift. Salvation. Grace. Freedom. Position. Love.

> A SINCERE *question* FROM A GRACE-BASED *leader* DOES NOT "CALL YOU OUT," BUT ALLOWS YOU TO *redirect*

A grace-based leader is a great question asker. When another leader asks me a sincere question about my own leadership or direction, it gives me an opportunity to save face, redirect, and rise to a place of integrity versus being called out or pointed out in a manner that is direct, humiliating and grows resentment. As uncomfortable as the conversation may be, it can usher in a necessary refining while providing me with an example of grace-based leadership.

I was a wife, mom and full-time business owner in my late thirties when I began to enter an important waiting season of my own. During the decade that I was having children, I never slowed down. I worked, wifed and mothered. Then one day God began to call me to stop working and stay home with my children. This wasn't an easy decision for me because

I've always enjoyed working. But I soon began to feel the discomfort of delayed obedience. When I was working, I felt I should be home. When I was home, I was preoccupied with thoughts of work. It seemed as though I was never enough for either area of my life. I struggled to prioritize what I should really be doing, and I constantly worried. I eventually obeyed and gave up my full-time job to be present with my children at home.

At first, it was great. I felt like I was on vacation, and every Monday morning I thanked God that I got to stay in my pajamas and do what I wanted. It wasn't long until I discovered that, in fact, I seldom got to do what I wanted. My expectations of life at home with four children, ten and under, were unrealistic and selfish. Even though I was with my children, I spent a lot of time finding something else they could do so I could focus on whatever else I deemed as more important. I was trying to do life at home disconnected.

After a while, I began to die to my expectations and embrace the reality all around me. I found contentment in caring for my family while letting go of many "to dos" I wanted to accomplish. I gained appreciation for the distinct personalities and gifts of my children, and I learned to be present.

Those years did more for me as a leader and mother than any other season in my life. I often state that it took four children and five years for the Lord to drive out selfishness. No title. No position. No business. No paycheck. I had no tangible, measurable leadership goal or result that was evident. Yet, I was reaping a far more glorious gift of a real and intimate connection with my children.

Never think that when you are following God's leading that the season was wasted time. Those years were forming the foundation upon which

I lead today. It was the character development and the relationship bonding that happened behind closed doors and in private that made me who I am today. The season of waiting was a prerequisite for future opportunities. It was a time to get my tendency to focus on tasks over people in its proper perspective.

Maybe you are experiencing a season that feels like you are wasting time, energy or resources. Maybe you feel stuck or even overlooked. Or are you dreaming of a future that you can't yet embrace? Sometimes we believe that our dreams are so important that they can't or won't happen unless we break free of the restrictions of our current season, the demands of our family or the limitations of other's needs. This is dangerous! God will hold you in a season until your character and relationships are ready to bear more weight.

Courtney Cohen, co-founder of Now Found Publishing and author of *Refining Identity: I Am Who I AM Says I Am* and *The Sacred Shadow: Enter Into the Daily Mystery of God's Kingdom,* shares about her own season of waiting.

> During this season of my life, I am in a place of greater obscurity. My primary leadership takes place at home with my children right now, though I know the Lord will bring me into other arenas in His time. To combat the discomfort of waiting, I begin with small steps, leading from where I am. This helps prepare me, moment by moment, to step into the greater vision and purpose God has for me without being overwhelmed by the waiting. For now, I am seeking to lead well where I am at in order to honor this assignment as well as prepare for future opportunities.

Rachael Gilbert is another gifted communicator. She's a business owner, counselor and host of a podcast, *Real Talk with Rachael*. I first met Rachael when she was participating in a leadership development experience with Gateway Women called WILD (Women in Leadership Development). That experience was impactful for her, not only revealing the next step in her leadership journey, but also bringing order and understanding into a season of course correction. That season highlighted the importance of hearing and obeying God regarding the timing and priorities we pursue. Here is her testimony:

> Several years ago, I was sitting in a discipleship class called WILD (Women in Leadership Development) at Gateway Church, when I felt God call me to start a blog. I had never considered myself a writer, but I started a blog anyway, fully expecting only my mom and aunt to read it. I soon discovered I enjoyed writing, and much to my surprise, other people enjoyed reading what I wrote. That little blog eventually opened doors for me to write magazine articles, speak at gatherings, and even launch a podcast.
>
> As my platform grew, I began to wrestle with the temptation to hustle. Well-meaning experts taught me the tricks of the trade but before long I lost the joy of the art of writing. It felt like a chore. I sought some counsel from a pastor at my church, who said something I will never forget. "Rachael, my motto is that if things aren't in order in my home, people shouldn't listen to what I have to say on stage." Her words put a spotlight on why I wasn't okay in that season. I had become so obsessed about what the outside world thought of me that I had begun to neglect my home, children, and marriage. That

day I took a few steps back and laid down some things I was leading in order to get my heart in the right place. For a few months I rested from my writing and let God heal me from getting affirmation from man. I am grateful for the grace-filled, yet, challenging words that leader spoke into my life. Without her, I may have continued to run full speed in a direction I did not need to go. Eventually God released me again to write and speak. Today, I enjoy a growing influence without sacrificing my personal life. Slowing down to hear, obey and wait on God gave me great peace.

It is good to wait upon the Lord for a season change. A delay does not mean never. God hasn't put you on the shelf or forgotten you. Let me say that again. God has NOT put you on a shelf or forgotten you! In God's timing nothing is wasted, and everything is preparation and pre-requisite to be trusted with His most important treasure—people.

Since the treasure of heaven—people—is at stake, it will be no surprise that the enemy of our souls—Satan—is standing ready to rush into your season of vulnerability. He will tell you lies that stab at your inadequacy and cast doubt on God's character and purpose for you. When you are most vulnerable, Satan will drive you to a self-promoting or self-protecting decision. He's not asking you to wait. He's pushing you to quit or to prematurely move forward.

This kind of spiritual warfare is always operating. Sometimes it gets into our souls and creates incredible dissatisfaction, fear and pain. Sometimes it's operating in the hearts of others who lead us. If their motives are not godly, you may experience some other ceilings I want to address. True discriminatory practices, injustice, racism, abuse or gender stereotyping must be brought to the light. I do not condone sexual harassment or abusive relationships of any kind. I grieve when I see women experiencing true oppression, bondage or betrayal.

These types of abuse are not glass ceilings. They are sin.

If you find yourself in a situation that is subjecting you to these sins, please speak up. Do not allow another person to dominate your body or spirit. Do not wait and hope for the best. Rather, be quick to find someone who can give you wise counsel and help you find the resources you need for help and healing.

I am about to introduce you to three secrets that are foundational to becoming a grace-giving leader. These secrets come straight from my heart, having been birthed and nurtured in a season of waiting. They are Scriptural. They are found throughout the lives of the people in the Bible. With awareness, you will be able to spot these secrets operating in the lives of those who lead with grace. I pray they impart to you the same grace that was given to me.

secret #1
GRACE EMPOWERS

Let's say you just finished your education. Since 16, you've been driving that old beat up car your parents bought for you. It's got a few dents and dings, a slow starter and tires that need to be replaced. It burns fuel like crazy and constantly requires upkeep. It's been known to fail to start and to leave you unexpectedly stranded. You can't wait to upgrade.

With a new job, a fresh start and a change of direction, suddenly you have the keys to a new vehicle. Your upgrade is significant. You take a few moments to admire its beauty, kick the tires, and set the seat just right. You click that seat belt and get ready to go. Up until that moment, everything has been imagination, observation and dreaming, but now it's time for power. You push the start button and a sudden rush of revelation courses through your mind. You can go anywhere. You have possibilities you didn't have before. You see the future and the road ahead from a new perspective.

Grace is like the starter button on your new car.

Grace is the key to power that makes everything possible.

It produces the ability, desire and power to change. It will transform your journey from the inside out. Grace calls out to us and invites us to connect with God through the work of Christ and by the presence of the Holy Spirit. The very appearance of grace can cause you to experience a sense of impending adventure. Grace motivates you to put your life in gear as you realize you are loved, valued and important to God and others. Your life has purpose, and grace is the avenue to accomplish your destiny.

> YET NOT I, BUT THE *grace* OF
> GOD THAT WAS *with* ME.
> 1 CORINTHIANS 15:10

I can't help but think of the woman at the well that Jesus encounters in John 4. Jesus invites her into a personal relationship with the living God. Yes, He addresses her past sins and religious concerns, but then puts the focus on the life He desires to give her. He gives her an opportunity to receive grace and power, and as she chooses to accept the invitation, her whole life changes in a moment. In fact, she was so changed from the inside out that we read, "Many of the Samaritans from that town believed in Him because of the woman's testimony" (John 4:39). She was no longer defined by her past or her circumstances, but by the love and grace of God.

> God patiently, by divine power, exchanges our weary and worn hearts with character that is healed, whole and full of grace. (Author Unknown)

While we are walking out this rather extensive metaphor, let's consider what's under your hood. What's the source of your power? Is it your own strength? Your goals? Your anger? Your greed? Even your righteous plans? What comes out of you when you press the starter button? Is it grace, or is it a counterfeit?

Comparison is a plain old counterfeit for grace that makes us believe that if we can just drive the most beautiful vehicle all will be well. Grace is not about the vehicle that you drive or the upgrades of your exterior life. Be careful that a beautiful exterior doesn't become more important to you than the source of power within. Both of the vehicles we just discussed had power. One vehicle had a rough exterior and the other had an external beauty. Yet we all know that the power comes from what is under the hood.

If you tend to constantly compare yourself to others, then you are in big trouble. Why? Because comparison is a killer of dreams. You will always find yourself better or worse than another, but you will never be satisfied with exactly who you are or where you are.

Here's what God's Word has to say about comparison:

> DON'T *compare* YOURSELF WITH OTHERS. JUST LOOK AT YOUR *own* WORK TO SEE IF YOU HAVE *done* ANYTHING TO BE *proud* OF. YOU MUST EACH *accept* THE RESPONSIBILITIES THAT ARE *yours*.
> GALATIANS 6:4-5 ERV

Comparison will hurt you, delay your dreams, reduce your effectiveness, and steal your joy. It puts your attention on the wrong things and strives to convince you that you are not okay or not enough. It says, "Try harder. Do more." It implies that what you do is more important than who you are.

Like any good counterfeit, it draws your attention by the promise of great reward at little cost. Don't believe me? Just think about how many knock-off designer purses are in the world. I picked up a few myself in New York and one time on the streets of Greece. I've even brought home a few from the port of Honduras, and I've ordered a wallet, sunglasses and a designer watch from somewhere in the Asian countries. Not one of those items has lasted long nor satisfied my desire for a quality item. I have given up finding a cheap substitute for the real thing, and I want you to do the same.

God is not into knockoffs. Don't be fooled anymore. It is Satan who is always counterfeiting the authentic gifts of God with cheap substitutes. God likes one of a kind original masterpieces. He values you so much that He is willing to invest in the business of restoration. He likes to put His touch on what seems to you beyond repair, forgotten or even worthless, and He touches it with His grace.

Maybe you feel like that old car, a bit beaten up and undependable. He doesn't just discard you or your pain, struggle or experiences. He doesn't trade you in for a newer model. He doesn't write you off and send you to the junk heap to be forgotten or abandoned. Rather, He injects grace into the divine character and calling within you. As a result, you begin to experience the power of His grace. He pursues us in our brokenness, replacing our self-sufficiency with His power and then patiently waits for us to manifest a restored soul.

When our engine—our character—is significantly transformed, we begin to display an exterior presence that is also beautiful. We are in a sense upgraded, empowered, and restored. Others might be drawn to a nicely refinished exterior, but ultimately, they want to lift the hood and look within. In a similar manner, lots of people may pass by your life, glancing casually at your exterior but making no real investment. It's those who feel drawn to connect with you that respond to the presence of God within you. When people connect to you and to the source of your power, they instinctively want to look closer and even experience grace for themselves.

I want to introduce you to Cynthia Baker. Cyndi and I work together at Gateway Church and have known one another for several years. She's always got a smile on her face and greets me with hug, but this year she participated with me and a small community of leaders in a six-week mentoring chat where we covered the principles of grace-giving leadership. As a result, I gained a closer friendship and a deeper knowledge of how grace has impacted her life.

Having moved to Texas in faith (that's a whole God story in and of itself), I did not yet understand that God brought me here for healing. My past is one filled with extreme abuse and dysfunction. My first days here in Texas were extremely difficult and my brokenness kept me in a victim mentality. Fortunately, I discovered a small group that would change my life. Despite my brokenness, never once did my small group leader shame or judge me for where I was in my journey. Instead, she came along side me, extended grace for me in my season and encouraged me to continue on in the hard work of healing. And that was no small feat. She taught me that when I am leading a woman God brings into my sphere, she may only be at the beginning of the journey I've already walked. Extending grace to them allows them to continue in that journey with no expectation that they need to have it "all together."

It was because grace was extended to me that I am where I am today. And it is in remembering my own journey that I can recognize where someone is in theirs and be able to extend the love AND compassion that grace calls me to extend. In doing so, I encourage a woman's walk, not hinder it.

Cyndi beautifully demonstrates the transformation that happens when we allow God to work on our engine. The evidence of the deep work done in the soul begins to manifest into something beautiful and grace-giving.

This transformation is costly. The authentic upgrade of your life will require a dying to pretense and self-help. Rather than polishing the hood, you'll have to open up the inner workings of your life and allow God to infuse you with a different experience. It is because the benefit is so great, but the cost is so high that many of us have fallen into a counterfeit trap. It's like buying the prettiest vehicle on the lot only to find out it's a lemon. We get caught up trying to be or at least looking like what we think others expect. We choose a way that promises results with less cost, less work and less time. We want the exterior beauty and the feel of power without the price of transformation. "The Lord does not look at the things people look at. People look at the outward appearance, but the Lord looks at the heart" (1 Samuel 16:7b).

It's when we stop focusing on what we wish we had or what others have that we can begin to truly appreciate who we are. Learning and embracing who you are and how you are fashioned by God is not a clear-cut process. It's an adventure of self-discovery and acceptance that slowly brings forth the best parts of your life.

Pastor Jen Weaver, who is my friend, co-worker, author of *A Wife's Secret to Happiness: Receiving, Honoring, and Celebrating God's Role for You In Your Marriage*, and pastor of women at the Southlake campus of Gateway Church, expresses this experience so well.

> No one fully knows what they're doing. We are all learning as we go along, asking God for help, trying to learn from our mistakes, and attempting new things we've never done before. If I were to begin again, I'd remind myself every day that who I am has been formed by God. My gifts and calling are irrevocable (Romans 11:29). I can't earn or disqualify myself from this identity. I must simply receive it as a gift.

The more I embrace my God-given identity, the easier it is to walk in it. You don't need to have it all together to be a trustworthy leader. Rather, just be you and carry the presence of Jesus with you.

Some of you are waiting for someone else to discover you and your gifts, and to choose you off the parking lot of life. You are waiting for a validation that you are worthwhile from another person who you perceive to be able to elevate your gifts and calling. The good news is that you don't need to wait on someone else to validate you. God already has spotted you. He is undeterred by what you perceive as insignificant or lacking in value. His focus is intent upon empowering you through grace so that you can experience His presence abiding in you. The only validation you need is the acceptance of God. He alone determines your worth and He alone brings the transformation that can catapult you into your destiny. You can trust God. Even when man fails, God will not.

> BUT HE SAID TO ME, "MY GRACE IS *sufficient* FOR YOU, FOR MY *power* IS MADE *perfect* IN WEAKNESS." THEREFORE I WILL BOAST ALL THE MORE *gladly* ABOUT MY WEAKNESSES, SO THAT CHRIST'S *power* MAY REST ON *me.*
>
> 2 CORINTHIANS 12:9

If you want the divine enablement of the Holy Spirit, then let me encourage you to accept the truth that without God we are all inadequate for the assignment. Without the grace of the Holy Spirit we remain uncertain and weak, "but with God all things are possible" (Matthew 19:26). Because He is full of grace, He will resist, hinder and even protectively hold you in a season of waiting until the secret, private, personal work of the heart can be successfully accomplished.

Christine Caine, founder of Equip and Empower, The A21 Campaign, and Propel Women, when asked how she does it all, said:

> It is the anointing of God. It is the divine enablement of the Holy Spirit. Life without divine empowerment becomes rigid and religious. It becomes very hard work. If you want the anointing of God to open doors for you, you must become more like him. (Episode 16 "The Process Is Painful." *Equip and Empower* podcast)

Just become more like Him. Spend more time in His Word. Practice daily worship. Learn to hear His voice. Devote yourself to His leadership. Make room in your life for the transformation of your soul so that you might experience the reward, the result or the transformation you desire. When you live your life this way, you will experience the promise of Acts 1:8:

> BUT YOU WILL receive POWER WHEN THE HOLY SPIRIT comes ON YOU; AND YOU WILL BE MY witnesses IN JERUSALEM, AND IN ALL JUDEA AND SAMARIA, AND TO THE ends OF THE earth.

PAUSE AND PONDER

Understanding the power of grace will change the way you think, lead and love. The more you grasp grace as a gift of empowerment, the more you will enjoy sharing it. The more you share it with others, the more joy you will experience. This is why we are beginning with this critical foundation. Learning to recognize, wait on and share God's grace is a sign of a maturing believer—a growing leader.

- Can you name a time when someone extended grace to you? How did it feel? What was the result?
- Do you agree with the statement, "Grace is the power that makes everything possible?" Why or why not?
- Have you been impacted by the counterfeit of comparison? How would you recommend an emerging leader deal with this concern?

secret #2

GRACE CONNECTS

Living in a state of connection is about learning to be present in the moment. This skill comes when you have confidence that God is mastering your life for His greater purpose. It comes with the conviction that the season you find yourself in is a needed part of your preparation for the future.

My husband and I recently began meeting with a counselor. After more than 35 years of marriage, four kids and now an empty nest, we wanted to do a little maintenance on our relationship and work on our emotional connection.

I was surprised when the first thing the counselor began to recommend was practicing being present. He wanted us to really focus on the moment, pay attention and grow still. We used our five senses to help us become present, thinking and saying aloud to one another what we could see, hear, taste, feel or smell. Sometimes it was awkward and even funny, but we persisted until it became easier. This exercise really helped us to bring a whole heart to one another. He helped us discover the grace that connects.

There are many rewards in learning to be present. When you are present with God, yourself or others, you honor them. Your breathing slows. Your focus increases. Your heart opens. In this position, you can experience true contentment and deep relationships. In this state, Philippians 4:11-13 ESV makes so much sense to me: " I have learned in whatever situation I am to be content. I know how to be brought low, and I know how to abound. In any and every circumstance, I have learned the secret of facing plenty and hunger, abundance and need. I can do all things through him who strengthens me."

The practice of being present is similar to grounding exercises. It helps when you've gone too far in your head and have lost a measure of self-control. It also helps if you are struggling to authentically express your emotions or hear the heart of another.

Practicing being present is simple. Start by breathing deeply for a few moments. Then, slowly bring awareness to:

- Things (the person) you see.
- Things you can touch.
- Things you can hear.
- Things you can smell.
- Emotions you can feel.

If you long to connect with another person or the Holy Spirit, you will have to go a step further. You will need to go from a focus on yourself to becoming aware of your surroundings, the atmosphere, and the other person. What is their mood? What are they saying, doing or sharing?

Ultimately, you will determine when and if it is safe to open a window to your real self. When two people practice this technique at the same time it can bring great breakthrough. Being connected in safety to another is a core need of the human soul. Ultimately, our human need is a mirror reflecting with great clarity our need to connect with God.

God is eternal. He's in the past, the present and the future, but you are only in the present. Therefore, if you want to connect with God, you must become present right now. When I am practicing being present in the moment, I settle down and become mindful. I turn my attention to God. I consider His Word; and I open my heart to the Holy Spirit. Inevitability, I become aware of His presence. Here I am safe. I can express any emotion, even negative ones, without retaliation or fear. I pray and wait. I know I'm ready to re-engage with the world when I am experiencing peace. I feel alive. Refreshed. Reinvigorated. I have a supernatural strength I did not have before. I experience the secret Paul mentions in Philippians 4:13 ESV, "I can do all things through Him who strengthens me."

Connection is so powerful that God chose it as a primary method of grace-giving.

Just think for a moment about how connected to God we become when we experience salvation. Christ redeems us. The Father accepts us. And the Holy Spirit comes to live within us. We are adopted into a heavenly family, and we are grafted into a family tree. We are endowed with every spiritual gift and blessing we need. All our debts are paid, and our sins are forgiven. We are connected intimately for all eternity. Romans 8:38-39 confirms our connection and speaks to our security. "For I am convinced that neither death nor life, neither angels nor demons, neither the present nor the future, nor any powers, neither height nor depth, nor anything else in all creation, will be able to separate us from the love of God that is in Christ Jesus our Lord."

> *connection* IS SO POWERFUL THAT GOD CHOSE IT AS HIS *primary method* OF GRACE-GIVING

Just like people connect to God through an awareness of His presence, people will follow and serve alongside a leader who is present and who walks in a grace that connects.

There is a saying that people don't care what you think until they know how much you care. I find that to be true. How do you demonstrate care? You connect. You reach out, send a note, make a phone call or, best of all, look one another in the eye and really listen.

This year, I connected on a deeper level with a dear friend, Emily Miller. I've known Emily for years and always experienced her as humble and willing to serve. I recently invited her to co-lead a mentoring chat on leadership development with me. We worked together to form an online small group of leaders. Emily was our point person, our small group leader. She was incredibly effective at bringing the group together week after week. She communicated often and well. She was always sensitive to the mood of the Holy Spirit and the importance of the topic of discussion we would engage that day. She got to know each person despite the fact that we weren't able to meet face to face.

Every week I was overwhelmed by Emily's grace. Not only did she care about the people, but she also cared that we would genuinely connect with God. She gave grace to me that was extraordinary. Every week she made a place for me to teach and to minister. I felt supported, loved and hopeful. I felt the weight of responsibility as a shared yoke, rather than a singular experience. I enjoyed her oversight and her leadership. At the end of our mentoring chat, I wanted to know how Emily became such an anointed leader. Here is how she answered my question:

> The answer to this question might be different from what you may be expecting or looking for, but the most influential mentor in my leadership journey has been my friend Jason. We co-led a life group together in college, and the way that he encouraged me to lead was really the launching point in my leadership. He affirmed the gift of God in me, affirmed that I had a voice and important things to say, and really gave me a solid footing for leading our group. I am forever grateful for how empowering he was because it was during those two years of leading together that I developed my foundation for leading others. That experience showed me how to elevate and honor those I lead and how to trust the leadership of God in my life. I learned so much about how to listen to others and how to create safe spaces for people

to share what is on their hearts. I learned how to collaborate and the importance of having fun together while leading.

Emily is a grace-giving leader. She took the secrets I'm sharing with you and embodied them. As a result, the leaders were tremendously impacted for good. Emily has our love, devotion and loyalty. The next time she has a need, these women will be eager to help.

You don't have to be serving in a leadership role to reap the reward that grace brings. As a matter of fact, I often spot an emerging leader because they are grace-giving when no one is looking. They already care and give grace to others through their actions, attitude and the atmosphere they create. They catch my eye because their character indicates they might be willing and/or ready to step out in a specific way.

I recently ran across an article by Dan Rockwell, founder of the *Leadership Freak* blog, that I feel embodies the simplicity of demonstrating care to another person. Simple caring actions such as these are humble in nature.

7 SMALL THINGS THAT MAKE A POSITIVE DIFFERENCE

1. Smile.
2. Show Interest. "How are the kids?"
3. Pat on the back.
4. Bring coffee for the team.
5. Celebrate progress and hard work.
6. Sing happy birthday.
7. Say thank you. (A smile and a little eye contact take "thank you" to a whole new level.)

Sometimes we disconnect and are not even aware.

Have you ever sat in a classroom trying to pay attention but only finding your mind darting in a thousand directions at once? Maybe it was from the moment you sat down, and you were wishing it were time to leave because you have so many other more important things to do. Maybe you are present in the body but absent in the mind. Maybe you are prone to daydreaming—reliving a conversation from earlier that day or planning ahead for tomorrow's meeting.

Almost by accident, we learn to drift, listen and connect half-heartedly. We are not present. We effectively close our hearts to others and communicate that being with them is not as important as being somewhere else or doing something else.

On the other hand, lack of connection leads to pretending, people pleasing, perfectionism and discontentment. Failing or refusing to be present with those you are leading creates a huge disconnect that screams of arrogance and breeds mistrust. You give off signals that are confusing. Your actions imply that others are not important and that you don't really want to invest in them. No matter how hard we work, it is never enough to bring us the satisfaction that comes with real connection.

> HUMILITY IS *friendly*, EARNS *trust*, AND PROMOTES *safety*.

The cure for such chasms is humility. Humility is friendly, earns trust, and promotes safety. It is open, trustworthy, and listens well. It is kind, quiet, aware, patient and makes room for others. It gives grace, shows honor, and accepts people for who they are. In short – it connects!

We find a powerful exhortation from Paul in Philippians 2:5-11: "In your relationships with one another, have the same mindset as Christ Jesus: Who, being in very nature God, did not consider equality with God something to be used to his own advantage; rather, he made himself nothing by taking the very nature of a servant, being made in human likeness. And being found in appearance as a man, he humbled himself by becoming obedient to death—even death on a cross! Therefore God exalted him to the highest place and gave him the name that is above every name, that at the name of Jesus every knee should bow, in heaven and on earth and under the earth, and every tongue acknowledge that Jesus Christ is Lord, to the glory of God the Father."

Much of the spiritual and natural battle we face involves keeping our mind and our bodies focused on the most important thing. Have you ever wondered what is the most important thing? "'Martha, Martha,' the Lord answered, 'you are worried and upset about many things, but few things are needed—or indeed only one. Mary has chosen what is better, and it will not be taken away from her'" (Luke 10:41-42).

I have so much empathy for Martha. I totally understand why she is frustrated with Mary, and I like to guess about some of the motivation behind her comments. It seems obvious to Martha what is most important in the moment. She is creating an environment that says to the Lord, "See, I care about you." I suspect Martha was a good cook and the older sister. She loved the Lord and wanted to please Him. She was so interested in making everything just right that she soon became frustrated and got annoyed with her sister's lack of help.

Yet Jesus doesn't fall prey to politeness in this moment. He knows that behind the blaming of Mary is an absent heart in Martha. Her mind, body and spirit are far away from the thing that is happening right in front of her.

What is that one thing that Mary chose, and Martha missed? Mary is present. She is focused, still and seated in the presence of Jesus. Her whole heart is open for connection. She is demonstrating the power of presence and, as a result, is rewarded by His presence—a connection with Him that "will not be taken away from her."

You can send the same signal as Martha to others by simply failing to be in the moment with them. Just consider how many times you've missed an opportunity to really connect because you were racing forward with a "to do" list or looking at your phone over dinner.

Leaders often fall into this trap. They have a drive to get things done that comes from right motives but are sometimes driven by wrong actions. This was Martha. Her motives for service were pure, but her actions spoke worry. More than that, when others didn't line up to her expectations, she both blamed and tattled.

PAUSE AND PONDER

Let's pause for a moment and just step back for a bit of perspective. Take a mental snapshot of your life today. Bring to the forefront your current work, your home life, your relationships and even the status of your spiritual development.

- How easy or difficult is it for you to really connect? What do you believe you need in order to connect more easily?
- How can the principles in this secret help you develop a wholehearted connection with God?

- In what ways do you need to embrace your current season or responsibility? Do you need to make any adjustments in your expectations of yourself or others?

secret #3
GRACE MATURES

Learning to wait on God's grace is a sign of a maturing believer—one who can delay gratification and wait for the best. When we wait, grace will deepen our roots and mature our character.

There is a really interesting story in Luke chapter 2 about Jesus. He and his entire extended family had traveled to Jerusalem for Passover festival, which was an annual activity for them. He was about 12 years old. He had been left behind by his parents after the holiday weekend. I can identify. I once drove off and left my boys at the library for a little while before I discovered my mistake.

I know it seems unlikely that they would lose a child. But, they would have been traveling in a big caravan of animals, people and belongings and were all headed out at the same time to a variety of destinations. At age 12, Jesus would have had some responsibility to keep up and probably to help with the younger children or animals. We learn in the story that he stayed behind on purpose, but his parents were unaware.

Joseph and Mary traveled an entire day toward home before they realized the situation. Then they spent another entire day searching the camp. Finally they returned to Jerusalem. They searched for three days.

That made a total of five days! I can't help but think about how panicked they must have been. They found Jesus in the temple sitting at the feet of the teachers asking questions and giving answers that were astonishing for his age.

At this point in the story, I can tell a man is recounting the event. With simple words and little drama, he tells us about the exchange between Jesus and his parents and leaves out so many details in Luke 2:48-49 I want to know. Mary said, "Son, why have you treated us like this? Your father and I have been anxiously searching for you." (Mary was upset! Me too!) Jesus replied, "Why were you searching for me?" "Didn't you know I had to be in my Father's house?" (Stunned silence.)

Even though we learn that Jesus "is about His father's business," we don't have any recorded words from Mary or Joseph. Does Mary grab him by the hair and march him out of the temple? Probably not. We do see a simple statement that says that Mary "treasured all these things in her heart."

The Scripture says they didn't understand what he was saying to them. Maybe they were still responding to the relief that he was okay and unable in the moment to process what he was declaring about Himself. At any rate, he went home to Nazareth with them, and then Scripture quietly records—almost like an afterthought—that He "was obedient to them."

We don't hear about Jesus again until He was 30 years old. Can you imagine what the years between 12 and 30 must have been like? Despite the divinity in Christ, they were a typical Jewish family. They had work, religious education, family celebrations, kids fighting, household maintenance, and daily meals. Jesus lived within an average family going about an average life until we encounter him again.

All we know for certain about the next 18 years is summed up in Luke 2:52, "And Jesus grew in wisdom and stature, and in favor with God and man." He grew intellectually and physically ("wisdom and stature") and in influence and grace ("favor") with God and man. Joseph and Mary mixed a home life devoted to God with the obedience that Jesus offered which produced spiritual, physical and emotional maturity in Christ. If Christ needed years of preparation in order to reach maturity sufficient for His calling, how important do you think it is for you and I? We also need spiritual, physical and emotional maturity in order to fulfill the call of God on our lives.

This is why grace is so important.

Jesus matured with divine grace and became an outstanding leader (and of course, so much more), and so can you.

God's grace will mature you. It will prepare you, and it will empower you. It will also make you able to be obedient and wait for the appointed time.

Even Jesus, who at 12 understood who He was and what He was to accomplish, waited for God's appointed time to step into His destiny.

Maybe the process of maturing is frustrating to you. You've been preparing forever, and you feel ready to advance. You might feel held back or unable to make a difference where you (are. You are waiting and watching for promotion.

Promotion is not the same as permission. God has already given you permission to practice your leadership skills right where you are.

Promotion belongs to God and comes only in His perfect timing and will. It is God's approval and timing that matters, not ours. God determines if and when you can be trusted with a higher rank or greater power.

Sometimes promotion will come as a surprise, and when it does, be careful to guard your heart from lies and fear designed to persuade you to self-sabotage.

LeeAnn Kirkindoll knows just what I'm talking about. LeeAnn is a leader, communicator and author of *24k Life: Living Every Day Refined By God's Word*. It is her heart's desire to enlighten women and girls of all ages about the importance of reflecting the light of Christ in their spheres of influence. As a leader and hands-on teacher in ministry, she's been a part of training, empowering and shepherding women entrusted to her for over 20 years. Yet, when a surprise moment of promotion came, she was tempted to let the moment pass her by potentially self-sabotaging her own call to ministry.

> I formerly served as a Director of Women's Ministry at the north campus of a mega church in the Dallas area. I can tell you with confidence, that the position—by the world's standards—should have never been mine. Although I had been leading Bible studies for years, I had not been to seminary—and I had no intention of adding a third degree to my resume! But as I prayerfully considered the position, God prompted me to write out a list of my life experiences that could affirm my ability to do the job. That part was easy to follow through on. I actually started to feel a little excited about moving forward. But soon after completing

it, the Holy Spirit prompted me to follow that list with the life experiences I felt might disqualify me. That, on the other hand, was zero fun. I bawled when I got through writing it. "What in the world are you thinking, God? I have made way too many mistakes to have a position like that."

However, by following through on that exercise, eventually God clearly revealed that my past heartbreaks and mishaps would actually be THE VERY THING that made me qualified to take on this ministry opportunity that now stood in front of me. Those areas where God extended grace to me would be the very same areas I would feel compelled to extend great amounts of compassion to others rather than judgment. My testimony could be proof of His desire to redeem and restore lives for His glory.

Peter's journey comes to mind here and how often we found him "jumping the gun" or getting ahead of Jesus. His devotion and passion were there from the start, but his timing needed work. As devoted as Peter was, he did exactly what Jesus said he would do, even though Peter was convinced he never would. Three times Peter denies knowing Jesus. And yet, there is glorious redemption in Peter's story! Jesus is not upset with Peter. When they meet again after the resurrection Jesus affirms the call on Peter's life and exhorts him to "feed my sheep" (full story in John 21). Then we are brought to Acts and all of a sudden it is Peter's time to shine! His training, waiting, and maturing process have brought him to this Pentecost moment where he boldly proclaims the gospel and "there were added that day about three thousand souls" (Acts 2:41). Talk about a powerful moment! This is where I find hope in the waiting season. I lean in and choose to trust that God is preparing me for greater works. "No one from the east or the west or from the desert can exalt themselves. It is God who judges: He brings one down, He exalts another (Psalm 75:6).

The word "exalt" is interesting. Some Scripture versions translate "exalt" as "lift up" or "promote." This is a good definition, but it also means "to make noble in character," "to dignify," or "to hold in high regard."

Therefore, promotion is an indication of your character development more than your ability. It's true that skills are required to lead but having skills without character is always hurtful to people. God puts a tremendous value on people, and He doesn't take abuse, neglect or selfish ambition lightly. Because He loves us, He puts us in positions that will develop in us the character traits of nobility, dignity and high regard for others. This takes time and obedience.

> PROMOTION IS AN *indication* OF YOUR *character* DEVELOPMENT MORE THAN YOUR *ability*

You can build worldly wisdom and favor with people by your own hands, but since you built it on your own, you will have to maintain it on your own. You will soon discover that this type of building is not enough to satisfy the human heart. It leads to disappointed feelings of inadequacy. What you need is to build upon a life of grace.

So, let go of your agenda and timing and simply lift your hands to receive His free gifts — salvation, mercy, peace, life, hope, power, connection, maturity, and grace. I could go on and on. There are many beautiful variations of His favor. If you watch closely you will discover the many characteristics (in addition to love) that mark the life of mature leaders. In addition to influence and favor, here are some additional examples of noble character that come from a life of grace. See if you can identify a leader who bears these marks:

- DIVINE POWER – GRACE
  My message and my preaching were not with wise and persuasive words, but with a demonstration of the Spirit's power, so that your faith might not rest on human wisdom, but on God's power (1 Corinthians 2:4).

- DIVINE HUMILITY – MEEKNESS
  Likewise, you who are younger, be subject to the elders. Clothe yourselves, all of you, with humility toward one another, for God opposes the proud but gives grace to the humble (1 Peter 5:5).

- DIVINE WISDOM – COMMON SENSE
  We do, however, speak a message of wisdom among the mature, but not the wisdom of this age or of the rulers of this age, who are coming to nothing. No, we declare God's wisdom, a mystery that's been hidden and that God destined for our glory, before time began (1 Corinthians 2:6).

- DIVINE REVELATION – VISION
  Where there is no revelation, people cast off restraint; but blessed is the one who heeds wisdom's instruction (Proverbs 29:18).

PAUSE AND PONDER

Character development is a life-long process of mixing grace with time and obedience. It produces the richness of heart that motivates us to care for others, to serve others and to empower others. God requires character development before He releases real responsibility for the care of others. Jesus grew in maturity so that He might be noble enough to lay down His life for others.

- Which of the characteristics of a mature leader do you feel you need to grow in? Is it wisdom, stature, authority, or favor? Ask God for more of His grace in this area of your character development.

- Do you agree with the following statements? "Grace will mature you, prepare you and empower you. It will also make you able to wait—to be obedient—for the appointed time." Why or why not?

- Make a list of the types of grace you have received from God. (ex: salvation, love, maturity) Spend some time acknowledging how these gifts of grace have helped you become a more mature follower of God.

> GRACE, BY *definition*, IS SOMETHING THAT GOD IS *not required* TO GRANT. HE OWES A *fallen world* NO MERCY.
>
> —RC SPROUL

chapter three

THE POWER TO CHANGE

She called me out of the blue one day. My quiet but faithful friend, Kristin Lemus, wanted to know if I would speak at an upcoming conference on the topic of grace-giving leadership. Of course I said yes because it was Kristin.

I really got to know her when I was in the middle of releasing my first book, *Women at War: Declaring a Cease Fire on Toxic Female Relationships*. Kristin somehow had gotten hold of the content. She was so sure that women needed to hear the message of how to create healthy female relationships that she reached out and offered to help me market the book. I remember the moment I realized she was an answer to my prayers. I didn't know then what a great mentor, friend and prophetic voice she would come to be in my life.

Kristin became a fast friend because she extended so much grace to me. She believed in a message that I held dear. She "got me," and more than that, we connected. We shared a mutual passion to lead with grace, to build others up and to empower those who God calls to lead and serve.

Kristin promoted *Women at War* to an inner circle of friends and followers who built a launch team and set in motion an online blog tour hosted by her friends. In 2013, I knew almost nothing about how the internet could extend and impact a message. I didn't understand the tools, the community or the influence that Kristin was offering to me. But I did understand that her heart was gracious.

The day Kristin called and asked me to teach on grace-giving leadership was another life-changing encounter with her. Everything in this book began out of the catalyst of that initial teaching. I showed up at The Declare Conference with my best ten tips in hand (see chapter 5). The truth is that the seed of those ten tips got into my own heart and began to bloom. No one is more surprised by the fact that I am writing on the topic of grace-giving leadership than I. Until that day, I had never considered the topic and I definitely did not call myself a grace-giving leader. However, I did work for and serve in a grace-giving culture that I believed needed to be shared. So, I said, "Yes."

Kristin is a forerunner for many. She has a supernatural eye that can spot anointing, gifts and potential. I am only one girl among many who have been so impacted. Maybe she is so powerful because of her unique perspective on reaching your dreams.

> God doesn't call us because we are perfect, know all that we need to know, or have figured out how to do everything right the first time. God calls us because we are willing to

say, "Yes," no matter what. He faithfully teaches us what we need to know along the way. We get to be imperfect and make mistakes. We even get to give up and start again. If you feel inadequate for the task ahead of you, you are not alone. Most of us do. Those who see their dreams realized are the ones who keep getting back up when they make mistakes and who keep trusting that God knew what He was doing when he partnered with them on their dream.

Kristin didn't just encourage me on day one. Over the years, she's read every version of this content. She's listened to my woes. She waited patiently while I delayed or gave up. And she often gave me a gentle kick calling me to gather the strength to keep trying. She truly is a picture of the power of a grace-giving leader. And what you hold in your hands is evidence that a seed planted in the heart of another can bear much fruit. She is a mother to many and a source of strength and power in every season of her life.

I am humbled by the opportunity to introduce you to Kristin. I long for you to know more about her dreams and the gift she is to weary moms. I asked her to share about her own journey of launching the Brave Moms ministry.

KRISTIN LEMUS

Tired. Weary. Overwhelmed. Most days these words hung over me as a mom. Guilt over what I had not gotten done and shame about what I thought I should be doing were constant companions. At my wit's end one night I asked God why I was such a bad mom without really expecting an answer. As soon as I said it though I heard God say:

> "Who calls you a bad mom? I call you a good mom. When I created everything, including a woman's capacity to be a mom, I stood back and called it good. If you will begin to believe Me and confess this as truth, you will become it."

That one encounter with God changed my life. I began leaning into the truth God spoke to me. I began to see how believing what God says about me helps me overcome weariness. This led me on a journey of seeking God's heart for me as a mom. That's when God led me to Joshua 1:9: "Be strong and courageous. Do not be afraid or dismayed. For the Lord your God is with you wherever you go."

As I read the verse I heard God say "This is my heart for moms. Read it again." I read the words slowly with tears coming to my eyes as I realized this verse wasn't just for a soldier in battle or preacher on the stage. It was for me as a mom, to walk out motherhood without fear and with strength and courage. I knew that if God said to be strong and courageous He would teach me how. I needed to trust God to help me through my mothering weariness so He would get the glory of the victories!

As I dared to imagine walking in confidence in my abilities as a mother, my mission became clearer. I had to stop fearing how my children would turn out and trust God. I had to make sure that the hardest days of motherhood didn't steal my joy or make me lose heart. I had to walk confidently in who God was and trust He was fighting for me.

This started out as my own journey but I came to understand that this was God's heart for all moms. This became the why behind the birth of the Brave Moms ministry. What God began in my own heart became a passion for me to share with other moms who were experiencing the same pangs of weariness. I didn't have to be perfect to do this, I just had to be willing. And I was willing to take God's hand and embark on this dream He had given me and start Brave Moms.

At Brave Moms, we help revitalize and empower weary and overwhelmed moms. We help moms know that God not only sees them but that He's crazy about them. We help them overcome fear and discouragement. We dig into God's Word together so they can know God's Truth. We give them hope. And our prayer for every mom is that they are able to leave weariness behind and walk confidently knowing that God is calling them to be a brave mom too!

Many of us have worn ourselves out trying to be perfect. Maybe like Kristin and like me, you have thought that perfection is a form of grace. Let me explain. Imagine "grace" as a woman. Her hair is clean, shiny, and perfectly coiffed. Her clothing is fashion forward and perfectly tailored. She turns the eyes of everyone in the room and seems filled with perfect peace.

Haven't we all strived to be this picture-perfect woman of grace? But is that grace or just a picture of grace we've been taught? We should all want to put our best foot forward when leading. Certainly, proper grooming and doing the best with what we have is important. Refining ourselves and what we put forward is never wrong. But striving to be this "perfect" woman can set us up to try and accomplish an impossible task. It is important that we be the leaders we're supposed to be—uniquely who God created us to be. And whether you're a perfectly put-together woman like the one described above or you're perfectly comfortable in jeans, boots and a t-shirt, grace is always much more about the character we display than what we wear.

And that character is built by allowing grace to change us.

Grace has many dimensions, but regardless of its manifestation, it always contains the power to change. And it will change you, if you let it, for the good.

The definition of grace we must hold onto is that it is unmerited favor. This is a form of grace you will want to discover. You can't work to earn it, though many have tried. You can't buy it, steal it, or duplicate it. It can't be copied, taught, or experienced by your own efforts.

Remember, it's a gift. "For it is by grace you have been saved, through faith—and this is not from yourselves, it is the gift of God—not by works, so that no one can boast (Ephesians 2:8–9).

Unmerited favor is what grace is, but it is what grace does that is so amazing.

secret #4
GRACE RECEIVED EMPOWERS YOU

Learning to seek and receive grace for yourself is a prerequisite to an overflow of grace that will empower others. When we receive grace, we begin a powerful journey of transformation. Grace produces the ability, desire and capacity to get the job done. It can unlock your dreams and help others unlock theirs. It equips you with a supernatural edge that enables you to address problems, empower others and build a successful, healthy life.

Receiving grace, whether from God or from others, empowers you with a supernatural, competitive edge to move forward, overcome obstacles and accomplish goals. Philippians 2:13 AMP confirms that grace empowers. "For it is [not your strength, but it is] God who is effectively at work in you, both to will and to work [that is, strengthening, energizing, and creating in you the longing and the ability to fulfill your purpose] for His good pleasure."

I have a simple, practical example of seeking grace for myself that shows how you too can draw on the power of God in your life. Not so long ago, I felt convicted that exercise was an essential key to help me cope with stress, regain strength, and improve my overall health. I knew this was true, but I simply couldn't seem to make myself exercise. I'd go through starts and stops over and over again. Although I knew what to do and I knew why I needed to do it, I simply lacked the power to do it.

> RECEIVING GRACE *empowers* YOU WITH A SUPERNATURAL, COMPETITIVE *edge* TO MOVE FORWARD, *overcome* OBSTACLES AND ACCOMPLISH *goals*

I began to pray. I talked to God about how I knew exercise was essential, and I confessed that I just didn't want to do it. I asked Him to help me want to do it. I asked God for the power to overcome my own resistance.

I prayed this prayer for several weeks, and then one day I thought, "You have a pair of shoes and a sidewalk. What is the excuse?" Immediately I felt the conviction that my excuses were many and my results were few. That day something shifted inside of me. Without another thought, I walked to my closet, picked up my shoes, and took my first walk. I'm not saying I didn't have to decide every day to obey, because I did. However, soon the benefits and pleasure of walking overtook my objections. I suddenly had a power—a will and an ability—that I had been lacking. "For it is God who works in you to will and to act in order to fulfill his good purpose" (Philippians 2:13).

I realize this is not a "wow" example of the power of receiving grace, but it does illustrate the truth that grace shows up everywhere—in the small things, the private things and in the large and public things. Once you recognize that grace is often knocking at your door, you can recognize it and receive it with joy because it releases power. It motivates. It challenges. It validates. It encourages. It believes.

I met my friend, Marilyn Weiher, many years ago. You could say we met across the table since my first memory is when we shared a meal with about 10 others. I watched, listened and learned. She intersected my life in a timely season when I first became aware that I was called to be a mother to mothers.

That word from God frightened me as I had a difficult relationship with my own mom. I had often felt disconnected. I felt I had lacked the kind of nurture a daughter might long for. As a result, I was just beginning to really understand and embrace the beauty of my own feminine strengths and stop rejecting my own identity. I was also learning to live in community with women and racing to figure out how to lead well. I was hypersensitive to the hearts of other women holding myself back from connection and trust until I felt safe.

Marilyn made me feel safe. She was and is a picture of grace. She was beautiful, elegant, wise and servant-hearted. During the first class she taught, she shared Psalm 139 from memory. That was so influential. She loved the Word of God and knew how to open the Scripture in a way that poured grace into my heart. I loved her from that moment forward. It would be a few years before I could share with her how much she planted in my heart over those first few days together.

Gratefully, over the years I found myself serving often with Marilyn. I watched her humbly step down so others could step up. She cheerfully made it possible for those who were watching to join in, to connect and to be blessed. She also impacted my daughter in a tender way loving her and recognizing the leadership call on her life.

Marilyn is, by profession, an educator. She also co-authored a book entitled, *The Home Experience ... Making Your Home a Sanctuary of Love and a Haven of Peace*, which she used in mentoring over 1,000 women in four-day intensives. Today she continues to teach and counsel many with great wisdom and care.

When I asked Marilyn who had been the most influential mentor in her life and how she was impacted, she shared that her leadership style was empowered by a godly leader. Here is her testimony:

> As a new believer during my undergraduate years in college, my most influential mentor was a woman named Fran. She demonstrated that mentoring is all about serving. She made a lasting impact upon my leadership style by teaching me the following truths:
>
> **Do as I do**
>
> As my mentor, she invited me into her life. I spent countless hours observing and learning from her while sitting at her dinner table, interacting and laughing with her family, and

watching as she honored her husband. I listened to her practical teaching, engaged in intercessory prayer with her, and attended church with her. I felt motivated to be like Fran because she joyfully led others by her godly example. The apostle Paul told the Corinthians, "Imitate me, just as I also imitate Christ" (1 Corinthians 11:1 NKJV).

Know who you are in Christ

Fran led with confidence being anchored in the Word of God. Convinced that God loved her, she trusted Him fully. She waited on the Lord, listened for His voice, and made sure what she heard aligned with the Bible. When dealing with hard times or difficult people, Fran persevered in prayer, love, and Scripture meditation until she felt peace once again.

A mentor's lasting impact

Passion, purpose, vision, and implementation all have their beginnings in a divine calling from God. Fran demonstrated that walking out your calling includes waiting on His timing, seeking wise counsel, knowing your own strengths and weaknesses, forgiving offenses, employing the expertise of others, and relying on the power of the Holy Spirit for continual guidance. Fran would say, "A man's heart plans his way, but the Lord directs his steps" (Proverbs 16:9 NKJV).

One of the most significant and impactful ways you can receive grace is through a mentoring relationship. Just consider for a moment that the apostles were mentored by Christ.

We can turn to them for some encouragement and affirmation because they experienced God's grace working through them in powerful ways. The apostles became great leaders. They not only established the early church, but also they even impact our lives today because they received grace and were empowered by it. "With great power the apostles continued to testify to the resurrection of the Lord Jesus. And God's grace was so powerfully at work in them that there were no needy persons among them" (Acts 4:33-34).

In the first four books of the New Testament we learn the apostles were a group of everyday working people who struggled just like we do. They became great leaders and experienced great grace after the risen Jesus gave them grace through the Holy Spirit. It was the grace they received mixed with obedience that transformed a ragtag group of men into the spiritual leaders we know today. "And with that he breathed on them and said, 'Receive the Holy Spirit'" (John 20:22).

The Holy Spirit is the greatest grace-giver. You can't really be filled with grace to the point of overflowing without the Holy Spirit breathing into you. He is the source of all grace and the first one in line to give it away. He is empowering. His grace flowing through you will ". . . testify to the resurrection of the Lord Jesus" (Acts 4:33) and work so powerfully through you that everyone around you will also be blessed. It's a beautiful, free-flowing gift given without limitation to those who love the Lord. It transforms us from weak and selfish to strong and powerful. The miracle

> GRACE *transforms* US FROM WEAK AND SELFISH TO *strong* AND *powerful*

is that we become vessels that are also grace-giving—overflowing—so that others are also empowered.

PAUSE AND PONDER

Once you understand how essential grace is to your ability to grow, transform or accomplish the impossible, you will earnestly look for opportunities to receive grace. You will sense that you are loved, valued and important to God. Let's take a moment and talk with God about your need for the kind of grace that empowers.

- Is there a situation in which you feel powerless or weak? How could positioning yourself to receive more grace change your mindset, situation or experience?
- Think of a mentor or two who helped you receive grace. What was it about them that made this possible?
- Identify two or three practical examples of ways that you can immediately be empowered. (Hint: The Holy Spirit is the source of grace.) What will you do to activate these ideas?

secret #5

GRACE GIVEN EMPOWERS OTHERS

I'm so excited about this secret because this is the "how to" of becoming a grace-giving leader. This secret is in the epicenter of the gospel and also right in the center of this book. The giving of grace to one another is a prominent picture running throughout the New Testament. Jesus was constantly giving out of what He had to heal, direct, save and influence others. The apostles also walked in this pattern, becoming fishers of men by offering the grace-filled good news to everyone. Consider Matthew 10:5-8:

> These twelve Jesus sent out with the following instructions: "Do not go among the Gentiles or enter any town of the Samaritans. Go rather to the lost sheep of Israel. As you go, proclaim this message: 'The kingdom of heaven has come near.' Heal the sick, raise the dead, cleanse those who have leprosy, drive out demons. Freely you have received; freely give."

When you receive grace, and the resulting authority that comes with it, you face a choice. You can resist the command to go and instead hoard grace, becoming spiritually fat and apathetic by failing to activate the grace you were given, or you can purpose to give away what has been given to you. You have the ability to limit the amount of grace you experience. You can lean upon your own strength, demand your own way, or try to prove something to yourself or others. Or you can lean on the strength that grace provides.

In Luke 6:38 we read these words from Jesus: "Give, and it will be given to you. A good measure, pressed down, shaken together and running over, will be poured into your lap. For with the measure you use, it will be measured to you."

I can see you're nodding heads now as I'm sure you've been discipled in the importance of giving from your resources and the power of tithing. But, have you considered that giving and grace are intimately tied together? If we look at this verse in context, we discover that giving is not just a matter of money or obedience, it is a matter of the heart. Let us look at the context in Luke 6:30-38.

> "Give to everyone who asks you, and if anyone takes what belongs to you, do not demand it back. Do to others as you would have them do to you.
>
> If you love those who love you, what credit is that to you? Even sinners love those who love them. And if you do good to those who are good to you, what credit is that to you? Even sinners do that. And if you lend to those from whom you expect repayment, what credit is that to you? Even sinners lend to sinners, expecting to be repaid in full. But love your enemies, do good to them, and lend to them without expecting to get anything back. Then your reward will be great, and you will be children of the Most High, because he is kind to the ungrateful and wicked. Be merciful, just as your Father is merciful.
>
> Do not judge, and you will not be judged. Do not condemn, and you will not be condemned. Forgive, and you will be forgiven. Give, and it will be given to you. A good measure, pressed down, shaken together and running over, will be poured into your lap. For with the measure you use, it will be measured to you."

Here's the bottom line. You get to choose what you give and what you withhold. When our heart is aligned with the heart of Christ we don't give to get nor withhold to control. We give to bless, and as a result, a blessing comes back to us. An unending cycle of grace is a resource of strength, hope, power and love for many.

This is so beautifully illustrated in Acts 3 by the story of the crippled beggar. Peter and John were approaching the temple to attend a prayer meeting. The man was sitting on the porch outside. When he saw them approaching, he asked for money. This was most likely the same request he made daily of every person who was entering the temple. On this day he had a supernatural encounter with a grace-giving leader that changed his life forever. Peter commanded the man to give his full attention to the two of them. Then he said: "'Silver or gold I do not have, but what I do have I give you. In the name of Jesus Christ of Nazareth, walk.' Taking him by the right hand, he helped him up, and instantly the man's feet and ankles became strong" (Acts 3:6-7).

What did Peter give to this man? He gave him the grace of healing.

A leadership that overflows from the grace that we have received from God is not a striving type of leadership or works based concept. As you and I encounter the living God we are transformed from the inside out. When we are filled with the hope and love of Christ, we can't help but pour that same love out to others. God did not send His Holy Spirit that we would live safe and comfortable lives, but that we would be moved to action sharing that grace and power to those around us. These are acts of grace. Grace comes and meets people in a time of need. It breathes life and hope into their hearts. I pray we would be the kind of leaders who allow God's grace to penetrate our hearts to the point that we would overflow to those around us and empower them to live grace-filled lives.

My long time friend, Wendy Moreland, has invested her life in the education field. She recently accepted an exciting promotion. Wendy, who started her career as a teacher in 1995 primarily with 3rd and 4th graders, was appointed as a coach to new and emerging educators and a mentor to developing teachers.

Wendy has always viewed her role as a teacher as a mentoring role ministering to children for a short season to invest skills, confidence, and love into each of their lives. Now she models that same grace-giving lifestyle to the next generation of educators ensuring that they too are benefiting from her experience and care. Wendy shared with me a little peak into her world and how she seeks to lead others with grace.

> As a mature teacher I press myself to constantly look for the good I see in young teachers (or even vets) around me. I will speak life over them privately, but there's something special about bragging on a young teacher in front of older ones. You can see that it gives everyone validation. The young teacher knows I'm sincere because I'm saying it in front of my colleagues. Also, the older teachers hear what the good was, and hopefully, they start looking for that good too either in the young ones or in themselves."

When you give grace to another, you empower them in a supernatural way. What seems small soon begins to have a large impact. The longer you expose them to grace, the deeper the transformation and the empowerment. Giving grace away is proactive. By its very nature, it begins with initiative. It is the person who will stand up first, speak up first or even reach out first that gains the joy of empowering others.

That's why people feel drawn to leaders who walk in grace. A grace-giving leader demonstrates a tenacious belief in the best version of who God created them to be. They refuse to let others live life aimlessly beneath the vision of God's highest plans for them. This leader is compelled to encourage and empower them to act on their potential and to help them become wholehearted and successful.

Here are some simple but practical ways to take the initiative in giving grace to others.

- **ELEVATE OTHERS**
  Take people somewhere they couldn't or wouldn't go without you.

- **GIVE TO OTHERS**
  Make it a priority to think about others more than yourself. Give away what you can of wisdom, opportunity, and praise.

- **RESPECT OTHERS**
  When others do well, extend your respect to them. They will respect you back.

- **MAXIMIZE OTHERS**
  Leaders like to follow leaders who will push them to be their best.

- **ADDRESS OTHERS**
  Don't be afraid to tackle tough issues. No one wants to follow a leader who won't address a problem. Be brave.

I personally experienced grace-giving in a transformative way in 2009 when I received a diagnosis of stage IV breast cancer. As I mentioned earlier, I was working as a part of the women's ministry team at Gateway Church. We were in a particularly busy season with many ministry projects that required attention. Soon after my diagnosis, I began to think about how the team would need to shift or change to keep up the momentum we needed.

At that moment, I knew what needed to be done. I would have to step aside and let others step up. Ministry deadlines would not yield to my circumstances, and as a result, I'd need to drop out or move to the side.

Yet, when I visited with my oversight, Pastor Debbie Morris, she had a different strategic vision in mind. She recommended we wait and see. She suggested we see how I did and then determine how it would impact my work. We could pause ministry and wait until we knew more.

We can pause. We can wait.

At that moment, I felt a sense of grace fill my heart. She made me feel that even though I might not be able to perform or lead, there was still a place for me. I felt so loved. It was amazing to just be washed in the full grace of being valued as more important than the work.

Over the next 18 months, I went through 19 rounds of chemotherapy, a full regimen of radiation, and a lumpectomy. I did not work every day, but I worked consistently. I also operated with more unity and a growing humility. I learned to allow others to help me. I let go of controlling every aspect of my work and made a place for others' input. Somehow, the ministry continued to move forward; nothing was left behind. God graced our entire team with an ability to accomplish more with less.

This experience changed how I lead more than it impacted my medical status. Now, I look for moments to really give another person grace. I am more secure, and I see weakness as an opportunity to give grace to myself and others. I am more patient and compassionate. I have greater empathy for a sense of powerlessness. I value others more and seek to make them feel safe. I don't merely cut people some slack. I don't flatter and exaggerate my trust in another's abilities. Instead, I use the gift of grace to teach people how to ask for God's help in every situation. I give grace away as often as I can, and I encourage with an authority that I've never known before.

Some people might fear this type of grace, thinking it is suggesting leniency, indulgence, acceptance of bad behavior, going easy on others or tolerating poor performance. They fear this grace will produce laziness, poor results, or ineffective teams.

That is not my experience.

When people are given grace, they are both humbled and strengthened. They experience a growing sense of love and loyalty. Their performance improves as their fear of public correction decreases. They are easier to lead, they grow stronger, and they learn to seek grace for themselves as a prerequisite to an overflow of grace that will empower others.

> WHEN PEOPLE ARE *given* GRACE, THEY ARE *humbled* AND STRENGTHENED AS THEY *experience* A GROWING SENSE OF *love* AND *loyalty*

PAUSE AND PONDER

People are fashioned with a need for grace. They flourish in the presence of grace, and they experience power when grace is given to them. You can become a dispenser of power by responding to others' needs and potential with the same grace that the Holy Spirit gives to you. When you lead as one who is full of grace, greatness will begin to appear in others all around you.

- Think of an example of when a leader gave grace to you to do something that seemed impossible or unreachable. In light of the idea that grace is the key to power, can you identify the moment they empowered you? If so, how did it change your situation?

- How would the impact of more grace in your own life effect your ability to give grace to others?

- What is it about you that draws other people? Maybe you are kind, hospitable, wise or caring. Identify a trait or two and contemplate how you can maximize that trait as a way to give grace to others.

secret #6
GRACE WITHHELD DISEMPOWERS

If we can learn to become a grace-giving, grace-filled, or graceful leader, we will naturally become empowered and empowering. By the same logic, if we become stingy with grace, hoard grace or become leaders who lack grace, we will become destructive—both to ourselves and to those we lead. Maybe you already know what I'm talking about. A lot of our relationship conflicts and pain are sourced from words, actions or moments of withheld grace.

Kristin Lemus, whom you met previously, shared with me about a conflict that arose unexpectedly in a mentor relationship and how the lack of grace brought so much hurt and confusion.

> After a few years of blogging, writing, speaking, and working on a team for a conference for Christian women communicators I had a discouraging encounter with someone who I admired and respected.
>
> During a conversation, this woman told me I was always trying to be seen on stage. The accusation hurt deeply because it was the last thing I wanted to be perceived as doing. I immediately asked God if it was true and if I was dealing with pride or a wrong attitude. I only felt misunderstood and wrongly accused.

I am interrupting Kristin's story to point out that disempowering grace is often wrapped in a package of a trusted relationship. This counterfeit counsel that discourages, disables and disempowers can be delivered as a fiery dart from someone you trust, respect, or look up to. Words came at Kristin in a moment in which she had no defense, no time or preparation to protect her heart, and no indication that she was about to be pierced. Now back to Kristin's story:

> I spoke with several trusted friends and humbly asked them if they would be honest and tell me if I did have a pride problem. Each one of them wholeheartedly refuted that accusation and assured me it wasn't what they saw in me. I even went back to this woman and had an extended conversation, but we couldn't agree on what was happening. In the end, I forgave her without resolution, but the damage was done. I felt hurt and wasn't sure what to do about it for a couple of years. Finally, I got up the nerve to share my lingering pain and resulting insecurity with a trusted mentor.

That was a breakthrough day.

This mentor spoke so much life and healing to my heart, sharing how that type of accusation manifests from a stronghold within the accuser. She revealed I was not wrestling with flesh and blood but against a spirit of accusation that wanted to silence my voice. She helped me understand how to overcome the accusation that came against me. She also ministered to me about how to see the person who had caused the hurt with greater clarity and wisdom so that I would know what to do in future situations.

I immediately felt as though a weight had lifted off of me and as if I could see clearly what had happened. I felt so empowered and encouraged after our conversation, and since then have been able to draw from her wisdom and advice to help other women who have been accused as an attempt of the enemy to squash their callings.

God used what was meant by the enemy for my harm and turned it around for my good and the good of other women I am called to serve.

There is a simple contrast between the two mentors that Kristin sought. The first one wanted to correct Kristin. The second one wanted to empower her. Trust is the foundation of any successful relationship, whether professional or personal, and when it is broken it is extremely hard to repair. We can't change the past or even change other people's minds, but we can receive healing and God's grace in these places of pain. Just as Kristin received healing and empowerment, God can meet you where you are to bring healing to your heart.

It's not selfish to receive God's grace for yourself, but it is selfish to withhold it from others. John 7:53-8:11 relates the story of the woman who was caught in the act of adultery. The scribes and Pharisees brought this woman to Jesus. We can almost sense their disgust with her and their desire for religion to prevail. But, Jesus showed her the utmost grace and compassion by somehow sending her accusers away. Some simple and yet powerful unknown words were written in the sand, and one by one they left. The woman's life was spared, and I can only imagine how this act of grace transformed her life. Here is a clear picture of what happens when grace is not withheld. Jesus could have easily done what was expected and allowed for the law to prevail. That was what everyone was expecting, but Jesus withheld the condemnation. He did not condone her behavior—we see his response to "Go now and leave your life of sin" (John 8:11)—but neither did He condemn her. Grace prevailed.

Wendy Walters is a well-seasoned and wise leader who is sought after for her preaching, teaching and worship skills. She is also an expert in providing publishing and branding assistance. She is a successful consultant, speaker, entrepreneur and the author of several books including *Intentionality: Live on Purpose!* She also created a workshop experience for first-time authors called *Release the Writer in You!* that has helped hundreds of people successfully cross the finish line to launch their dreams.

Wendy and I have been friends for years. She was one of the first leaders to help me discover and articulate my own dreams. Many times, she's sat me down, asked a few key questions and then given me a strong nudge to move forward again. I've seen her do the same for countless others. My heart was especially broken for her when a couple of years ago she and her husband walked through a ministry transition season that was extremely painful and certainly felt unjust. Here, Wendy shares a little about the emotional journey that led them to a greater trust in God rather than in man.

> A few years ago, my husband was let go from a job he loved, had diligently sought the Lord about before accepting, and that fit him like a hand in a tailor-made glove. In the months that followed, our whole family experienced the aftershocks of the trauma. Each time a new person heard the news or reached out to check on us, it triggered the emotions in us too raw to stabilize between blows. During that time, I sought the comfort and counsel of a dear mentor.
>
> She had been in my life for years, modeling for me how to interrogate a problem and scrutinize the circumstances. From her I learned to ask my problems:
>
> **Why are you here?**
>
> **Why have you shown up in my life at this time?**
>
> **What blessing do you hold for me?**
>
> But in the middle of this crisis, I had forgotten these things. Instead, I wanted resolution. I wanted an apology. I wanted someone who was involved to acknowledge that what happened was really crummy and just say they were sorry.
>
> One particularly overwhelming day I was walking around an outdoor garden at a hotel speaking with my mentor on the phone moments before I was about to show up and share from a pulpit. My insides were a mess. I did not know how I was going to show and minister love and hope with such

unresolved hurt in my heart. I have never been a plastic leader. I have always shown up authentically. Yet here I was, bruised, broken and bitter, ready to run, hide and lick my wounds.

I will never forget the way she responded to me. Without missing a beat, she playfully answered in her best southern drawl; "Praise God from whom all blessings flow, my dear, and thanks be to God who always causes us to triumph."

I was stunned. The hot tears streaming down my face turned tepid. Maybe she didn't understand how hurt I was. Maybe I had not communicated the level of betrayal I felt or the uncertainly of the future that lay before us. I must not have conveyed my anguish at the turmoil I saw in my husband's countenance.

Her voice turned softer. "Now listen, free will is an interesting thing. All men have one and all men—even good men—fumble the ball now and then. That free will they exercise sometimes collides into yours, and no matter their intentions or how much they feel they are in the will of God, sometimes they hurt you. Sometimes you hurt them. Some things are just plain unfair. This thing you are experiencing is hard, and right now, you are miserable. But, darlin', don't waste your sorrow. There is not one thing you can do to change what has happened or undo what has been done. What you can do is hand this thing over to God and step into the finished work—the already done factor—of your future. You love the Lord; your husband loves the Lord. You are called according to His purpose, and that guarantees that this thing is going to work out for your good."

I felt the breeze touch my face, and when I blinked, no new tears leaked out. I felt strength pour into me as she spoke truth to my spirit and reminded me of who I was, and the plans God had for me.

Wallowing was useless but my pain has purpose.

What could have turned into a festering pool of bitterness that would keep me from trusting leaders ever again, or risking covenant relationships, was lanced that day on the phone with my mentor. She put the axe to the root and cut off the work of the enemy from taking a foothold in my spirit. Of course, healing is a process. Of course, it took time before things turned around for us, and we charted a new course and adjusted our journey. I took that pain to the altar again and again and again, each time coming away with a bit more healing, a bit more perspective, a bit more hope.

Good leaders are not flippant when you come to them in crisis. But neither do they comfort what needs to be killed—your flesh. She spoke truth to me, and called me up into who she knew I was as she reminded me of what I carried. God would never leave me or forsake me. Men will fail, but God never will. She pointed me back to the Father and nudged me into receiving His loving care. That's what grace-filled leaders do.

All kinds of experiences will happen to us in this life, many of which are beyond our control. Some will be difficult or maybe even unfair, unjust or damaging. You can easily make judgments and speak curses about the motives of those who hurt you. You may even get trapped in your own lies and frustration, deciding to punish them as a means of communicating your disappointment. That won't make you feel better. The good news is that your ability to heal and recover comes down to how you handle your own heart.

I want to shine the light on another person who often withholds grace and disempowers—and that's you. How often are you the one that limits your potential—or the potential of others—because of distraction, fear, or offense? Most of us don't need another person to stop us in our tracks. We are quite capable of demoralizing ourselves and unknowingly rejecting the grace that God is eager to give.

LeeAnn Kirkendoll, who I introduced to you previously, shares about a personal experience where her own response to offensive behavior could have crippled her impact and relationships.

> The biggest regret I have is regarding my first "official" ministry leadership job. I was prone to let the behavior of others affect MY reactions in certain situations. I wish I would have been less "offended" and more aware of how much grace I could have been "caught extending" by not allowing myself to be rocked personally by another's choice to be disingenuous. No matter what happens in your leadership tenure, you always have the choice to rise above disappointing circumstances and people. That is where your true power as a leader lies. The goal as a leader is to REFLECT JESUS. He did not let another person's poor behavior and attitude change His mission or the legacy He would leave.

If you find yourself in a situation that leaves you brokenhearted, please find a wise friend who will lead you away from disempowering blame and finger pointing and steer you toward forgiveness, hope and peace.

Overcoming self-sabotage in high intensity moments or times of disagreement is another challenge for each of us. Pastor Jen Weaver shared the following wise words with me about operating in grace during conflict:

> I often defaulted to seeing conflict as a problem itself, instead of recognizing conflict as an unearthing of the actual problem. This causes me to avoid or delay hard conversations or refrain from sharing how I feel about something because I don't want the tension to escalate. A grace-giving mentor in my life has continued to help me see the value of healthy confrontation and the fruit of courageous conversations. She's taught me that, like in most things, handling courageous conversations well takes practice.

Just think of all the opportunities Jesus had to withhold grace from the disciples, but instead, He chose the opposite. Jesus had a bigger vision—the Kingdom of Heaven. And this vision was to bring abundant life through His saving grace to all who would choose it. So, rather than withholding grace, let me encourage you to take on the character of God in these situations. God is so patient with us and will allow our mistakes to season our experience with wisdom. When you have the opportunity, empower someone else rather than tear them down. "For the LORD God is our sun and our shield. He gives us grace and glory. The LORD will withhold no good thing from those who do what is right" (Psalm 84:11 NLT).

Our God covers our mistakes. He forgives. He teaches. He is grace-giving.

PAUSE AND PONDER

If you will choose to wait until your emotions have subsided and then approach a problem, a mistake or a misunderstanding with a grace-giving attitude, you will have a chance to salvage a difficult situation. You may be able to change failure into learning.

- What is your tendency when something goes wrong? Do you tend to add punishment to those who fall short of the mark, or do you tend to give grace? Can you give an example of each?
- What could you do to restore trust in a relationship that has been damaged? What could you do to help prevent a loss of trust?
- Think of a time when someone extended grace to you. Then think of a time when someone did not. Contrast and compare these two experiences, and see if you can find some practical tips for the future.

> GOD'S *grace* AND *forgiveness*, WHILE FREE TO THE RECIPIENT, IS ALWAYS *costly* FOR THE *giver*.
>
> —TIMOTHY KELLER

chapter four

THE POWER TO INFLUENCE

My husband and I were on the verge of becoming empty nesters and would soon celebrate our 35th wedding anniversary. Our daughter was only weeks away from getting married, our oldest son had just gotten engaged, our middle son was a college student, and our youngest was about to graduate from high school.

As our daughter's wedding date was drawing near, I was spending extra time with her friends, watching their relationships, and enjoying hearing about their plans. They were so incredibly gifted and full of vision and dreams. They already possessed a sense of destiny and purpose, desiring that their lives be ones of impact and success.

They also had many concerns.

They were anxious about juggling successful careers and family life. Some were working hard to overcome things that seemed to stand in their way and trying to process the pain that came from their upbringing, life experiences or even their own insecurities. Perhaps they were even frustrated by the difference between their leadership abilities and their leadership assignments.

My heart leapt with a bittersweet joy as I watched them. Though they were anxious, they were leaning into community, relationship and shared goals as a means to strengthen and encourage one another. It seems most of us need a little extra encouragement when it comes to our dreams.

Since women have always held positions of authority and influence, I can't help but wonder why we still struggle so hard on a personal level about where, how and if we should be pursuing our dreams. Women have always been among those who have led the charge in shaping and encouraging the next generation whether as entrepreneurs, community developers or mothers. Today, it is acknowledged that women can be both mom and CEO—leader and follower. She can lead from a place of being single or married, and she can even be a pastor or president. The choice is hers.

This expanding awareness has revealed new and creative opportunities for women. It can also reveal confusion and even some fear around whether we can or should be leading. Many women who want to, or even must, lead outside their homes or communities struggle with the sensation of dueling demands. They mentally divide their life between work and home, feeling torn between their passion for their personal lives and families versus their desire to make a greater impact in the world.

There is nothing wrong with a desire to be influential. I believe in developing a competitive edge, an entrepreneurial mindset and the desire to become a top leader in your industry. But, I also believe the highest levels of leadership success are found in working together with others both to overcome our fears and to do something significant with our lives. You can develop wisdom to make great choices and to lead yourself and others well. Whether you are a stay at home mom investing in the leaders at your feet or starting your own business and working tremendously hard to lead a team, the choice of when and how to lead is yours. Whatever your decision, watch out for your own harsh judgments—and possibly for harsh judgments from others. If you have to justify your choices to yourself or others, you can experience a tremendous sense of dissatisfaction, guilt, anxiety, or maybe even anger. You may feel called to something more while feeling confused or misunderstood.

It is possible to put God and family first while simultaneously leading in other roles or positions. Women do it every day all over the world, and so do men. So, don't be too hard on yourself, quick to speak rudely about yourself or to downplay your gifts and experiences. Don't beat yourself up for what you are not able to do or for feeling the weight of your responsibilities. Instead, begin to ask God for more grace, ability, desire, and power to do what you have committed to do.

> IT IS *possible* TO PUT GOD AND FAMILY *first* WHILE SIMULTANEOUSLY *leading* IN OTHER ROLES

In the end, what matters most is your heart, your calling and your willingness to honor God's timing in your journey. Are you at peace with your decisions?

Then move forward with joy. Is the timing right for advancing? Then get busy. Are you in unity with those who are partnering with you? Then it's permission granted. Don't let a lack of grace for yourself or from others be the reason you live stressed out, guilt-ridden or unfulfilled.

My own leadership journey began with lots of dreams, goals, and a deeply rooted wrong belief that I could lead well by navigating alone. I am an only child. Frankly, I didn't know any other way to navigate. I was used to thinking, deciding and acting on my own. I looked for a sisterhood, a community to do life with, but I was looking in the wrong places and for the wrong reasons. With my eye on the goal but without a support team, I often felt uncertain and misunderstood. I was wide open spiritually to every lie and fear because I lacked both trust and community in my relationships. I was immature, and my spiritual foundation was full of problems.

A faulty foundation in any building will eventually be revealed through the shifting and cracking within the finished structure. Maybe the windows stick or a door won't close. Perhaps tiles break or cracks appear in the walls. When these symptoms begin to emerge, a wise builder will walk outside and search the entire structure for leaning walls.

The parable of the wise and foolish builders found in Matthew 7:24-27 and Luke 6:46-49 so clearly illustrates my experience. I was foolishly building on sand. I kept resetting the structure and beginning again only to find myself discouraged, alone and even wiped out by the circumstances of my life. I didn't realize the importance of building my life on obedience to the teachings and examples of Christ who said:

> "Therefore everyone who hears these words of mine and puts them into practice is like a wise man who built his house on the rock. The rain came down, the streams rose, and the winds blew and beat against that house; yet it did not fall, because it had its foundation on the rock. But everyone who hears these words of mine and does not put them into practice is like a foolish man who built his house on sand. The rain came down, the streams rose, and the winds blew and beat against that house, and it fell with a great crash" (Matthew 7:24-27).

When your foundation has become unstable and cracks begin to appear in your life, you face a choice. You can either patch the symptoms of your fears and keep right on trying out of your own strength or you can go straight to the root problems and experience restoration.

Kristin Paschke has helped so many people, including me, put their fears in proper perspective and overcome them. She leads so well because she is always pointing those she loves to hear and heed the voice of God. Like a trusted mom, she can embrace your pain, comfort your heart and still point you to the power source you need—Jesus Christ.

> It's my opinion that at one time or another, we ALL battle insecurity, comparison and fear. Insecurity and comparison travel hand in hand. Once deception is recognized, I personally need to hear the voice of the Lord assure me of what is true. I often share my own struggles, with how I war against my flesh and battle darkness. I find that being transparent validates the other person's experience and helps them to receive truth. I am grateful I have friends that call me out when they hear me compare myself or believe a lie that allows fear a foothold.

The Holy Spirit continually reminds me that it's not about me and that my call is to point people to Jesus. Insecurity, comparison and fear only happen when my eyes are upon me.

Maybe some of your fears and their consequences are as obvious as mine. A lot of people dread public speaking or worry that their written skills are lacking. Maybe you are anxious about decision-making, or you are unsure how to ask for help.

My fears went way beyond doing well; I feared being really known and rejected. Truth be told, I was hiding from being known by God. I was wise in my own eyes but foolish in regard to the ways of God.

I can testify that it wasn't until I had a life-changing encounter with Christ coming at a moment of total surrender, that my own eyes were opened to the depth of deception and fear I was battling. When I put my eyes on Jesus and looked fully at my fears, I was able to give up being the leader of my own life. I finally tasted the sweet sense of security that is a grace gift of God, and the cracks in my foundation began to repair. I started to listen to and obey the wise Builder. The Word of God and the awareness of the Holy Spirit gave me a sense of safety and purpose I had not known. I also overcame that terrible sensation of being alone.

> THE *Word* OF GOD AND THE *awareness* OF THE HOLY SPIRIT WILL *give* YOU A SENSE OF *safety* AND *purpose* YOU HAVE NOT BEFORE *known*

Dr. Cassie Reid, founder and owner of Cassie Reid Counseling, is a marriage and family therapist, educator and entrepreneur. She owns a thriving private therapy and counseling practice, and she also serves as the Dean of Marriage and Family Therapy at The King's University. She is also a teacher, conference speaker and author of *Unwrapped: Open the Gift of Holiday Sanity*. Cassie has successfully run her own business, works within a non-profit education organization, and still finds time to mentor and encourage so many people. In her work, she sees the impact of insecurity and fear on our dreams.

> I think most people struggle with insecurity, comparison and fear. It is what you do with it that will determine your level of leadership. You have the power to decide if you will let it rule you or you rule it. I think the enemy loves to come with insecurity and comparison to give us an open door to disqualify ourselves. Fear is something that no one wants to wrestle with, but overcoming it can most definitely propel us into a place, position or even relationship we were designed to discover. I feel like the things I fear are the things that I should lean into the most.

I've been finishing the final edits of this book in the midst of the Covid-19 pandemic. During this season, I've been prayerful about the future and the ministry of encouragement and mentoring I am trying to shape and share. I have often felt overwhelmed by all the steps, decisions and actions required to share what is meant to be a gift. One day, seemingly out of the blue, I got an email from a lovely young woman named Marisa Donnelly. She had come across my website. Something in the message of women empowering and supporting one another grabbed hold of her heart. Marisa is a creative and articulate writer, editor, writing coach and founder of Be A Light Collective. During our very first phone call she introduced herself as a clarity coach helping others move from where they are to the place of their dreams. As I've gotten to know Marisa and as she's invested in helping me shape my message, I've also gotten to know a bit about her journey. I've gained a greater understanding of why she is so passionate about helping people connect and share their visions.

> I have a vivid memory of sitting in a coffee shop when I was about thirteen or fourteen, pouring my heart out to my mentor. She was a woman of grace and strength. She saw me for me and didn't judge me for the past, the path I was on, or even the truths that I shared with her—even the truths I had not shared with anyone else. What I loved most about this woman was that as she helped me unpack my trauma, she wasn't quick to give me a suggestion or even an answer about what I should do. Instead, she simply looked at me and saw my worth. Only then did she help me see myself through the lens of my Father whom I was forgetting amidst my pain. I felt seen when I was with her.
>
> I think that's the most important and valuable thing about mentorship—someone seeing you. I stepped away from that conversation knowing that I wasn't emotionally stuck, even though my physical situation remained the same for a while longer. She gave me a voice, a push, and a reminder I needed to re-center back on the truths of my heart and my God. I am thankful for her vision and guidance and can only hope to inspire others as she has inspired me.

My heart squeezes a bit as I feel the pain that Marisa was experiencing, but I am also celebratory that a wise woman was leading her to restoration.

Did you know that grace is restorative?

God will take the rubble of your life and rebuild your foundations. He doesn't just restore; He builds. He will use your God-given gifts to connect you with others who are also being restored. Look for the people who are restoring lives and modeling grace with great influence and integrity, and do as they do. "You'll use the old rubble of past lives to build anew, rebuild the foundations from out of your past. You'll be known as those who can fix anything, restore old ruins, rebuild and renovate, make the community livable again" (Isaiah 58:12 MSG).

One of those influential restorers I know is Amy Ford. Amy is the co-founder of Embrace Grace, a non-profit organization that exists to inspire and equip the church to love on single and pregnant young women and their families. It was at a Pink Impact conference that the call to "love the mommas" was birthed in Amy's heart. I have always felt such a sweet connection to Amy and the Embrace Grace community simply because I was present at the moment of birth and have had the honor of an up-close witness to her step-by-step obedience to God.

I hope you won't miss the significance of the organization's name—Embrace Grace. Long before I was understanding the power of grace, Amy was receiving it and giving it away. When I am tempted to doubt my own calling or to revert to a comfortable pattern of doing it alone, I remember that my friend, Amy, never carries the vision by herself.

AMY FORD

When I was nineteen, I had an unplanned pregnancy. Fear overwhelmed me and I came within moments of having an abortion, but ultimately, ran out of the clinic and courageously chose life. I and the baby's father (now my husband) were so close to losing our precious son because of fear—because of isolation, shame and feeling that there was no one who would understand.

All my friends left one by one. Looking back, I know it wasn't because they didn't like me. They just didn't know what to do. Our pregnancy was "the elephant in the room." People didn't know whether to say "Congratulations" or "I'm sorry." In the end, they didn't say anything at all.

Before getting pregnant I was very active in the church and had a lot of friends there. After getting pregnant, I tried going back to church, but things had changed. No one acknowledged the pregnancy and the baby growing inside me. It was as if they couldn't see me. For some, it was hard to make eye contact. I felt invisible.

So, I left.

It wasn't until years later that I had the courage to try church again. God healed my heart while at a ministry conference I was attending. And then, He "dreamed down" a heavenly inspired idea to start a small group at my church for single women with unexpected pregnancies. Even though I felt terrified and unqualified to begin a group like that, my heart came alive at the thought of it.

Our first Embrace Grace group launched at Gateway Church and three mommas showed up. At the beginning of the twelve-week class, they were without hope for their future. They felt as if their lives were over. By the end, they were excited and empowered to be the moms God created them to be. Our mission became clearer by the minute. These girls needed to embrace grace and be embraced by grace.

Love had transformed them.

The vision God had given me was no longer only in my head. It was standing right in front of me.

Each semester more and more women came. Then interest from other churches grew and wanted to start support groups as well. Before long, Embrace Grace was blessing mommas we had never met as baby showers and support groups spread from city to city. God was building something much bigger than this small group at Gateway Church, and we knew it. He was starting a movement of love among believers that would travel beyond cities and spread from nation to nation. Through Embrace Grace, He wanted us to encourage the global church to be a refuge for the broken hearts of single and pregnant women. We believed He wanted us to turn what had begun as a small group for three discouraged women into a nonprofit organization that could inspire and equip churches all over the world.

Embrace Grace is now in over 700 churches, 47 states and 10 countries.

Amy is a wise builder and an anointed leader. She may have started with a shaky foundation but quickly found the love of God that leads to restoration. Today her influence is significant. Amy has saved and restored the lives of countless young women and their babies. She has also introduced them to the body of Christ, led them to salvation and freely given them grace. As a result, God has opened doors within the church, the government, local community organizations and, maybe most significantly, in the hearts of thousands of people around the world who believe that every girl with an unplanned pregnancy can have a church to go to for spiritual, emotional and physical support.

Amy tells us to just begin our own journey right where you are.

When you hear God speak, simply obey. If you don't know what to do, just serve where you are. If you don't have a vision or dream of your own, then help someone else fulfill theirs. You don't have to wait for some super moment. You should begin now. Starting today, let's spend the rest of our lives making other people feel less broken.

> LET'S SPEND THE *rest* OF OUR *lives* MAKING OTHER PEOPLE FEEL *less broken*

So how do you find that grace-giving leader who can help you begin the process of restoration? Just begin right where you are. She might be living, working or serving right next to you. Maybe you will find her in the pages of a book, an article, a blog or a podcast. You could encounter her at your local coffee shop, community gathering or church.

Several of my friends shared with me about their own most impactful experience with a restorative leader. Take time to notice where and how these relationships were built.

> I've been blessed to be surrounded by many influential leaders at Gateway Church. During a time when I was struggling with leading women, one woman stands out. I noticed Gaye was shepherding many young women, and I asked the Lord to arrange a way for me to get to know her. He did! She taught a women's group in my home for a year. During that time the Lord prompted me to be still and watch. I quickly recognized that every woman had something valid to share and needed confirmation.
>
> The Lord continues to sensitize my life to how important it is to stop and listen to men and women. I've also learned how to gracefully interrupt, re-route and affirm without being abrupt. Gaye called out greatness in everyone! She listened as women shared and looked at them as though they were the only person in the room. I knew it was Jesus in her life that I was drawn to, so I wanted Jesus BIG and foremost in my own life.
>
> I appreciated her willingness to be transparent with her own difficult seasons and situations and I emulated a sensitivity to share my own stories when led by the Lord. Gaye recognized my deep love for prophecy and desire to learn more. She always encouraged me to share what the Lord was saying even though I heard and ministered differently than she did. I'm constantly amazed and grateful for how the Holy Spirit reveals His heart and opens opportunities to call out leadership,

destiny, & identity—all because of her mentorship (Kristin Paschke).

Interestingly enough I have had a few significant influential mentors in my life. The common denominator that they all share is their ability to see gifts in me and selflessly call them out. They were willing to speak truth to me, make a way for me, and cultivate giftings that I did not even see in myself. Watching each of them lead differently, yet with such impact, has shaped my leadership style today (Dr. Cassie Reid).

The most intentional mentorship I had lasted two years with an older woman from my church in Colorado during my newlywed/new mother season of life. She intentionally poured into me as I tried to discover my identity apart from being a student. Until that time, I had found my worth and value in accomplishments—particularly grades.

But, in a brief period of time, I moved across the country away from family, got married, settled in a new church, went through pregnancy, and had our first child. One thing my mentor did very well was asking good questions. This allowed me to grow in self-understanding as opposed to simply being told by yet another elder what I should do. Coming into my own personhood during that time, she played a valuable role. I take her method of asking good questions into my awareness today wherever I lead. Though it's tempting to simply provide the "right" answer, if I begin with a question, the person I encounter can often come to the best conclusions themselves.

In addition to questions, I make sure that I've been given permission to speak into a person's life. If I have not been entrusted as a safe sounding board and voice into another person, I must discern when and whether to speak because my words could do more damage as that person builds even higher walls of defense. Be safe for others. Ask good questions. Ensure permission to speak freely. These all honor the people we seek to invest in (Courtney Cohen).

Don't forget to look at the most important mentoring tool we possess, the Bible. There are so many role models within its pages. Don't be fooled thinking you can't relate to their stories. Our circumstances, seasons, and roles may vary from moment to moment, but the emotional, relational and spiritual challenges we all face are timeless.

Marilyn Weiher teaches on some incredible examples of mentoring relationships in the Bible that show us how to view and wisely value the restorative leaders in our lives.

> The Bible offers many profound models for mentoring. Three outstanding ones are: Elijah with Elisha; Naomi with Ruth; and Paul with Timothy. What can we learn from these great mentors and mentees?

Remain committed and faithful to the one who is mentoring you.

- Elisha remained by Elijah's side (see 2 Kings 2:2, 4, 6). God blessed Elisha for his faithfulness and for his teachable spirit.

- Ruth remained faithful to Naomi, her mother-in-law saying, "Don't ask me to leave you and turn back.

Wherever you go, I will go; wherever you live, I will live. Your people will be my people, and your God will be my God" (Ruth 1:16 NLT).

- Timothy demonstrated his faithfulness by not only fulfilling the apostolic assignment Paul gave him, but also he welcomed the instructions given to him in Paul's letters (1 Timothy and 2 Timothy).

Willingly serve the person who is mentoring you.

- Elisha was Elijah's humble servant.

- Ruth served Naomi purely out of love for her.

- Timothy became Paul's traveling companion and co-worker fulfilling important assignments that were entrusted to him.

Seek a spiritual inheritance from the one who is mentoring you.

- "Elijah said to Elisha, 'Tell me what I can do for you before I am taken away.' And Elisha replied, 'Please let me inherit a double share of your spirit and become your successor'" (2 Kings 2:9 NLT). The Lord granted Elisha's request.

- Naomi rewarded Ruth, her widowed daughter-in-law, by seeking ways to restore her life. She instructed Ruth to continue working in the field of a kinsman redeemer named Boaz. Without questioning Ruth obeyed her mother-in-law's instructions, which eventually led to her marriage to Boaz. They became part of the lineage of Christ.

- Paul prepared Timothy for a great spiritual inheritance by equipping him for the tasks of ministry, empowering him for success, and by communicating his love, respect, and support for Timothy—even calling him his "dear son."

It is a weighty matter when you realize that your leadership will impact the lives of others, and therefore, it must be carried with much wisdom and grace. So, let's slow down for a moment and spend some time examining what healthy leadership does and does not look like.

The next two secrets are so critical to your development as a grace-giving leader. Maybe you heard the quote by John C. Maxwell who says, "Leadership is influence—nothing more, nothing less." Everyone has some level of influence. But just because you have influence doesn't mean you are a good leader. There is so much leadership advice and counsel available to you today. How in the world do you sift through all this chatter to find the foundational wisdom and counsel you really need?

IT IS A *weighty* MATTER WHEN YOU REALIZE THAT YOUR *leadership* WILL *impact* THE LIVES OF *others*

Sometimes it is helpful to highlight what is true by first identifying what is false and misleading. Therefore, I'm going to begin by sharing with you about some myths and misconceptions about leadership. These lies need to be completely eradicated from your tool belt. Some of them are downright dangerous. All of them lead to frustration, dissatisfaction and loss of influence. Once we've established what leadership is not, we are going to get down to the Biblical values and definitions of what leadership is really all about. My goal is to be sure your foundation is established on a healthy understanding of the purpose and power of influence.

secret #7
LEADERSHIP IS NOT ABOUT YOU

Intentionally trying to grow as a leader can become an obsessive practice I call "navel gazing." It's easy to become focused upon what we know, do or think. We can become confident in our experience or gifts and become self-obsessed giving more weight and value to our own journey than to the people we are leading.

We must find the balance between self-awareness and self-obsession. True leadership is execution based and focused on turning our attention toward others rather than self. Knowing ourselves is important, but valuing ourselves over others is unproductive. To break a cycle of self-sufficiency, remember why you are leading and how important others are to the objective. Look at them; not at yourself.

What we've been learning all along is that leadership is not about us. It's about how we can empower others and lift them up on our shoulders.

LEADERSHIP IS NOT ABOUT GENIUS.

GENIUS: *exceptional intellectual or creative power or other natural ability*

Sometimes, especially in educational or intellectual pursuits, we put a huge value on intelligence, genius and brilliance.

It helps to be smart. It helps to be educated. It helps to have real world experience. These things may open doors of opportunity for you but none of them—in and of themselves—are going to qualify or ensure your success as a leader. They are helpful tools. They are good resources. But intellectual power is not the same as leadership. You can be very intelligent and lack the qualities of a good leader.

I'm going to spend some more time in the next chapter sharing with you about the value of your intelligence and the proper perspective on what you know, so I'm going to keep it brief right here.

LEADERSHIP IS NOT ABOUT POSITION.

POSITION: *a place where someone or something is located or has been put*

Leadership has almost nothing to do with a position. Though seniority in an organization or a title that implies responsibility may be an indicator that someone has leadership skills, it does not guarantee that a person will rise to prominence or effectively lead a team.

We tend to think of leadership as a position, a role, or an activity, and sometimes ones that seem denied to us. We don't believe we are a leader unless we can identify a public responsibility that requires us to hit the bull's eye of a project.

I want you to obliterate this type of thinking from your mind. True leadership is not an if/then proposition, nor is it tied to a particular season, position, or responsibility. No assignment will suddenly make you a leader. Generally speaking, titles, assignments and positions come to those who have been identified as already leading in their current sphere of influence.

LEADERSHIP IS NOT ABOUT FAME OR VALUE.

> FAME: *the condition of being known or talked about by many people, especially because of notable achievements*

Along the way you may receive some fame, fortune, or public recognition, but you can never count on the approval of man. You cannot—you must not—seek to determine your value based upon the praise of other people. I don't think most of us sit around and dream about fame. We usually think that fame is for a few and not for us.

Maybe fame is not your goal, but rather, you long for affirmation that you are seen and appreciated. Your value is based upon others acknowledging your contribution or highlighting your success. Either way, you must settle who you are and whose you are before you will be able to handle the public recognition of a successful leadership endeavor.

Public recognition will never fill our need for acceptance. If you are leading from any place in your heart that still needs nurture, affirmation, acknowledgment or love, I am doing you a favor by letting you know these needs can only be met through a personal relationship with Jesus Christ. Even if you gain public renown, you will still long for what others can't provide.

LEADERSHIP IS NOT CONTROL OVER OTHERS.

CONTROL: *to domineer over, act arrogantly toward*

Jesus talked about this type of leadership: "You know that the rulers of the Gentiles lord it over them, and those who are great exercise authority over them" (Matthew 20:25 NKJV).

So much of the leadership we see in the world looks like "lording it over" others. Life presents us with plenty of opportunities to practice this type of leadership. It is full of selfish ambition, desire for control, and is rooted in forcing others into cooperation.

If people follow you as a leader only because they have to, then they will do only what they are required to do. I know this is not your goal. People never give their best to someone they like the least. They will give reluctant compliance, but not commitment.

PAUSE AND PONDER

I found that upon reflection I had believed some of these myths, and as a result, I was hindered in my own development. I was focused upon the wrong outcomes. Once I intellectually understood the truth, I began a journey of recalibration. I am hoping you too can clear up any misconceptions that might hinder your leadership potential.

- Can you identify a common misconception you've had about leadership? How has this affected your journey?

- Have you ever experienced a leader who tended to "lord it over others?" If so, how did you respond to this leader? What advice would you give to someone currently in this situation?

- In what ways are you redefining leadership? Pause now and have an honest conversation with someone you trust about what you are learning.

secret #8
LEADERSHIP IS ALWAYS ABOUT OTHERS

Let's explore what true leadership really looks like. We can start by looking at the way Jesus finished his teaching on leadership in the Gospel of Matthew saying, "It shall not be so among you. But whoever would be great among you must be your servant, even as the Son of Man came not to be served but to serve, and to give his life as a ransom for many" (Matthew 20:26–28 ESV).

Apparently, the leadership style of "lording over others" has been around for a very long time because Jesus clearly felt the need to redefine being a leader as being a servant. Leadership is a responsibility to serve. It is a privilege—yes—but a responsibility first. You are being entrusted with an opportunity to invest in people, not just projects. It's not just about what you are doing, but more about why and how you are doing it.

LEADERSHIP IS ABOUT BECOMING A SERVANT.

SERVANT: *a person working in submission to another*

You have a duty to model care for those you lead. Jesus didn't just talk about leadership; rather, He modeled it. He is the chief of servants. Everything about His life is serving. His whole leadership development program is based upon a "come, follow me" style of compassion and service to others.

What if your title isn't CEO or Executive Director or Marketing Representative or even Mom, but rather Chief Servant?

Hear me. This is the most critical truth you must grasp. Leadership is service in its purest form. When you sign up to lead, you are not just agreeing to some position on a flow chart of an organization. There is so much more at stake.

Everyone on the organization chart under your name should really be positioned on your shoulders—above you. You are taking on a responsibility of service to those you lead. You build them up. You develop their skills. You address character flaws. You control the pace of their assignment. You give them the right to minister to others. You are their encourager and their safe foundation. We should humbly consider how we can strengthen our own character in order to stand firm under the weight of leading. "Each of you should use whatever gift you have received to serve others, as faithful stewards of God's grace in its various forms" (1 Peter 4:10).

You and your gifts are fashioned to administer God's grace by meeting needs. An administrator ministers by dispensing, giving, providing, or distributing gifts of grace as needed. Those gifts might be resources, tools, training or a title—but they also might be encouragement, responsibility, authority, and grace. You oversee the execution and use of those gifts to accomplish a goal, meet a need, and serve a person. Ultimately, you are responsible for teaching others how to lead as a servant.

This is when you become a leader of leaders—a servant of servants.

LEADERSHIP IS ABOUT FOLLOWING.

> FOLLOWER: *one who accepts the guidance, command, or leadership of another*

In today's culture of massive social media influence, we care a lot about how many followers, likes, or shares we are getting on our latest posts. We often build our own following by becoming a follower of someone else we esteem or value. This can be misleading you to building a confidence in a following that is uncommitted and unconcerned.

Remember that people can be fickle. Jesus rode into Jerusalem on a donkey, with palm branches waving and shouts of "Hosanna!" Just a few hours later, the same raving fans changed their minds and turned on him, screaming, "Crucify Him!" Your security is in God alone and not in your followers.

I love to read through the Gospels and notice how Jesus selected his own leadership dream team. Time after time, he used the simple invitation of "come follow me." He didn't say, "Come do what I tell you."

Today, we've taken that same vernacular and turned it into a push button, quick response and limited commitment key on our phone. We are often failing to grasp how important it is to really recognize, acknowledge, and follow a good leader. More importantly, we don't understand that our first responsibility is to be a good follower.

Everyone answers to a higher authority of some kind. Realizing that even the highest level of leadership responsibility comes with a corresponding oversight and accountability helps you to value the experience of learning to follow well.

Following well is an indication that you are ready for greater leadership. Jim Collins, author of *Good to Great,* teaches that if you want to be a great leader you must also be a great follower.

Following is more important than leading.

following IS MORE IMPORTANT THAN *leading*

Every follower buys into and supports someone else's vision before they have the experience, credibility and maturity to ask others to support them. Actually, this responsibility never leaves. You should always be investing in someone else's dreams. This doesn't mean your dreams aren't important, but it does mean that learning to submit and serve another's vision is a critical part of leadership development.

It probably won't surprise you that the same character traits that apply to great leaders also apply to great followers. Great leaders model them, and great followers acquire them. This is why who you follow is so important.

Your ultimate leader is Jesus. As a follower of Christ, you are intimately engaged in a relationship where you are invited to become a follower. As you walk together, you soon begin to acquire His character and to think like He thinks. You invite others into this following. Soon, you lead other followers and introduce them to a way of life that is transformative. Suddenly the saying, "Follow me as I follow Christ" (1 Corinthians 11:1 MEV) becomes truth.

LEADERSHIP IS ABOUT AUTHORITY.

AUTHORITY: *the power or right to give orders, make decisions, and enforce obedience*

Now maybe I am getting down to what you thought leadership was really all about. This is definitely what I thought leadership was about when I was a little girl. My mom tells a story about me coming out of kindergarten, jumping into the front seat, and proudly announcing that I could run that place if someone would just answer the telephone for me. I thought I was big britches enough to give orders, make decisions, and enforce obedience.

The longer I live and the more I lead, the more I realize I have so little wisdom to really wield the sword of authority. I find myself constantly before the Holy Spirit asking for the grace to walk in the authority that is upon my life. I no longer want to tell people what to do. Rather, I want to help them hear from God for themselves and obey. I don't value making decisions so much anymore. I'd rather watch and coach another to make a great choice that aligns with God's will and blesses others. I hate enforcing obedience. It's simply no fun.

Can I be really honest at this moment? So many times, I want to tell someone what I'm about to tell you, but their heart can't hear it.

You won't be a great leader or part of an effective team if you have issues with authority. Your leadership and its impact will be greatly hindered.

In Mark 6:7, we learn that Christ sent out His disciples with the authority to overcome impure spirits. When we set out to serve (lead) others with the right motive and attitude, God places a divine authority upon our word and work. It comes to us with an equal measure of responsibility. Authority issues point directly at a lack of trust in God as our Father. When we yield (submit) to an authority (to God and those He appoints), we yield our trust.

Most problems with authority happen in our lives because someone in authority abused our trust. I am so sorry if this has happened to you. I am doubly sorry if you have abused someone else's trust. People are broken, and they will fail you. But the authority that comes from our relationship with Christ is based in love, not abuse. We must allow God to heal our hurts so that we can submit to Godly leadership, Godly counsel, and Godly wisdom.

Sometimes God simply breaks our desire for authority and teaches us to embrace the simple message of trust and submission. Learning to wait quietly for God to speak or lead is a great sign of spiritual maturity, and it springs forth when you trust God with your whole heart.

> YOU WON'T BE A *great* LEADER IF YOU HAVE ISSUES WITH *authority*

This understanding and proper position in relationship to authority might be the single most challenging leadership test of your life. Authority is a fragile tool in the hand of a leader. Abuse it and it will hurt you. Love it, share it, and carefully weigh it, and it will draw you and others to a greater impact.

LEADERSHIP IS ABOUT TEAMWORK.

> TEAMWORK: *the combined action of a group of people, especially when effective and efficient*

True leadership is a lifestyle that requires a laying down of your life and a lifting up of the lives of others. It's not just about advancing yourself; it is about advancing with a team. If you follow well, you will soon be entrusted with greater assignments. If you lead others well and help them to become effective leaders, you will be successful at influencing and impacting others for a good purpose. That's because true leadership is a team sport.

You and I are in partnership with God. No question, He is the CEO, but you have a primary role to play as well. God refuses to build His church, expand His Kingdom, or make Himself known without the help of mankind. We partner with God and others to accomplish a divine mission, the Great Commission. You and God are a team. Your family is a team. Your marriage is a team. The church is a team. We are surrounded by potential teams. None of us ever have to be on the field of play alone. Isolation and self-protection are enemies to your leadership dreams.

PAUSE AND PONDER

Our western mindset always builds a hierarchy of leadership that is narrow at the top—a design where *many people support a few*. Biblical leadership is like turning that structure on its head where *a few people support and build up many*. As you understand what leadership is really about, you begin to understand why it is not only a privilege, but in fact comes with a great deal of responsibility. If you lift others up on your shoulders—lifting them higher into their own leadership journey and giving them power through grace—you will become a leader that others love to follow.

- Jesus invited His apostles—and ultimately us—to follow Him. This is still His strategy for team building. What principles about growing your team could you draw from the importance He placed on inviting others to follow Him?

- Is there someone you are following who isn't going the same direction as you? If so, why are you following them? Are there some changes you might need to make in order to align yourself with a leader who shares your values or goals?

- Are you in partnership with God? If so, you have a big responsibility to accomplish a divine mission. How will you build the kingdom of God based upon what you've learned about what leadership is really all about?

> By God's *grace*, I'm *learning* to ignore the crowds and *live* for an *audience* of one.
>
> —KIRK CAMERON

chapter five

THE POWER TO LEAD

In this chapter I will be sharing two of the most powerful secrets to becoming a grace-giving leader. They are simple and straightforward, but they are not easy. They require a true selflessness that is rare today. They will test your motives and your mantle of leadership. They are full of grace but lack any pretense. You can't fake them. They operate from the heart and are truly anchored in the foundation of service. The more you embrace them, the more likely you are to reach the pinnacle of your leadership influence.

At the pinnacle of your journey, people will follow you because of who you are and what you represent more than for what you do. Your character, knowledge, and skills will all come together to attract people who want to experience who you are. They want to be a part of your team and they want the kind of grace that marks your life.

You will know you are becoming an effective grace-giving leader when you see those you lead not just following but learning to lead others. A leader of leaders is more than a leader. They are influencers, authentic culture changers, catalysts for growth, and beacons of wisdom. John Maxwell calls this level of leadership, "the pinnacle of leadership."

> To become more than "the boss" people follow only because they are required to, you have to master the ability to invest in people and inspire them. To grow further in your role, you must achieve results and build a team that produces. You need to help people to develop their skills to become leaders in their own right. And if you have the skill and dedication, you can reach the pinnacle of leadership—where experience will allow you to extend your influence beyond your immediate reach and time for the benefit of others (John Maxwell: *The 5 Levels of Leadership: Proven Steps to Maximize Your Potential*).

I am so fortunate in this season of my own leadership journey to be able to say that I have walked with several pinnacle leaders. The exposure to those—who have been diligent, persevered past hardship, disappointment and challenges, and still find themselves daily ready to engage and lead with wisdom—has radically impacted my life.

One of those women is my friend and "sister," LoriAnn Biggers.

LoriAnn is the co-founder and CEO of BellaVaughn, an award-winning global diamond and design company with collections exclusively distributed worldwide through BlueNile, Inc, a Bain Capital Company. She has over 25 years of experience in the global finance and insurance industry, notably in executive roles as President of Lloyd's of

London for North American, the Navigators Group and Wells Fargo, Inc. Today, she still serves on a number of international corporate boards.

It's her motives behind the work that speak to me about her character and her purpose. She is passionate about the defense of civil liberties and the protection of abused and exploited women and children. She teaches ethical business practices to leaders and entrepreneurs. She serves on the non-profit boards of Equip and Empower, the A21 Campaign and Propel Women where she works to abolish human trafficking and to train and equip leaders for global impact. Her community service activities are of paramount importance to her.

LoriAnn entered my world at a critical moment and with a big splash. I had just been diagnosed with Stage IV breast cancer about 48 hours before our conversation. Hardly anyone other than my boss had even been told. I was smack in the middle of the threat of death and searching for a strategy and a team to help me overcome. I was rattled.

It was a Friday afternoon in June, and I was in the office alone. I was sitting at my desk when the phone rang. I was surprised to realize I was speaking with LoriAnn. I had already heard about the female executive leader who had joined Gateway Church. She radiated both authority and kindness and was clearly a mover and a shaker.

I was a little intimidated when I realized who I was speaking with. I was professional and tried to be brief but helpful. I wanted to honor her and engage with equal enthusiasm, but I felt like hiding. I didn't want her to know how weary, fearful or weak I was feeling in the moment. I was "all business" leaning toward hiding behind a calm, collected and helpful demeanor.

LoriAnn was having none of that. Within just a few moments she began to break down my barriers. She stepped right over my guarded heart and began to speak directly to me. She said God spoke to her about me and that we were going to become sisters—real friends. I don't think I ever mentioned my diagnosis to her on that phone call, but she believed for both of us that we were going to be friends for the rest of our lives. She was so sure, but I was not. Looking back, I can now say with confidence she was right. Something significant did indeed form between us on that day.

LoriAnn proved to be a woman of her word within a very short season. She just kept coming back to my "wall of doubt" and pouring out a little more grace onto my torn heart. There have been so many times over the years when I would have allowed this relationship to drift to a place of polite ending because I was insecure. Despite what I perceived as vast differences between us, she just set her eyes on the goal and did not give up.

I'm sad that I operated in such a self-protective way for so long. I was so busy being afraid of rejection, abandonment or appearing weak that I missed many opportunities to just be her friend. Even though I know practically nothing about her fields of industry, what I do know is that she is a leadership development dream. She comes alongside a leader—whether of great or small responsibility—and she gives grace. She sees potential. She discerns the heart. She boldly calls out your gifts and generously shares herself.

LoriAnn wasn't connecting to me because I had anything to offer or even because she was thinking she could teach me something. She simply listened to the Lord and acted upon what she sensed. God has used her to help heal that overbearing insecurity that worked so hard to help me hide, and to encourage me countless times on my health journey.

It's not a one-sided relationship. To my surprise, God has also spoken to me, and over the years, I have offered my friend a discerning heart, a listening ear, a faith-filled insight and an appreciation for the spiritual warfare that surrounds a leader of leaders. I love her for who she is more than for what she does. I am pretty impressed with what she does, but it is the heart behind the action that wins me over every time.

LORIANN BIGGERS

From the time I was a little girl, I just naturally stepped into positions of leadership. When I was in kindergarten, I would stand on the chair and direct, teach and rule the room. I was tutored at home by my grandmother in how to be a woman of God. Every day she would lay out photos of our family on her bed and we would kneel to pray for them. She made sure that this girl was centered in a life of faith in Christ.

My dad was a successful entrepreneur who helped me develop a mindset and work ethic that has been foundational to my success. He always told me, "You can do anything you want." He cast a vision for me to believe I could do anything.

Education was a priority and I began my college years as a music major. My sophomore year, my father suggested I might broaden my focus so that I would have a fallback position in case the music industry failed to be lucrative. So, I did. I studied music and mathematical sciences, with a focus in finance.

I began my professional career learning the auto industry and eventually went to work with my dad. Soon I was trying new roles and learning about risk assessment and management. That led to a career in the finance and insurance industries. I've had the privilege of working with some brilliant people and for several great companies, but about 10 years ago, my priorities and focus shifted significantly. I actually walked away from what some would say could have been the biggest job of my life. At the peak of my leadership, I just knew God was intervening in my plans, calling me and my husband, Keith, to live with more purpose and intentionality.

I shifted industries and got in touch with my creative design side. I launched into a whole new global field of diamond jewelry design and distribution through a company I co-founded called Bella Vaughan.

It's not all been by just my hard work. Much of my success lies in my dependence upon Christ. I have always had a supernatural awareness of His presence, and I have sought to make decisions and to obey His spirit. He has comforted me through many challenges—health crisis, infertility, divorce, blended family, and constant demands and temptations of a corporate lifestyle. My faith is the foundation of my life.

I have also been significantly impacted by the examples of many influential mentors. We all need an example to follow—someone who embodies the values or character we ourselves hope to demonstrate. Even the Apostle Paul confirms this truth when he said, "Follow my example, as I follow the example of Christ" (1 Corinthians 11:1).

One of my most impactful mentors was a gentleman who held major influence in my industry. I learned so much just by watching him be an authentic and consistent leader of leaders. He showed me how to carry myself and how to interact with people—not just ones who seemed to have the power—but also with the ones who served or supported. He was gracious in receiving honor and kind in giving it to others. He was consistently the same regardless of who was in the room. To this day he is the gold standard of leadership for me because of how he treated people.

I have a second mentor who embodied a lot of the same attributes, but—on top of that—I was working with him face to face each and every day. He had a great ability to know when to insert himself into issues and when to let people figure out how to deal with the messes they made on their own. He functioned like a good father, giving all of us enough leeway to learn to walk on our own, but never so much space as to allow us to injure ourselves or others. He was so incredibly prepared for meetings. He raised the bar of leadership for me. I learned how important it was to show up ready so that I could contribute effectively in the decision-making process.

Today I am in the legacy building mindset. I feel called to use my experience, influence and energy in ways that either empower others or bring hope and healing to broken lives. I am especially concerned about the issues of human trafficking, international human rights and the opportunities and development of more women at senior levels of leadership.

I'm expanding my business, investing heavily in problem-solving opportunities that impact people, loving on my co-workers and friends, and cherishing this season with my home and family. I am grateful for all the

> I FEEL *called* TO USE MY EXPERIENCE, INFLUENCE AND ENERGY IN WAYS THAT *empower* OTHERS

opportunities that were granted to me and for the grace to receive and share the love of God.

Recently I was speaking with LoriAnn, and we were discussing the ideas and content of this book. She had several great ideas and experiences that I just can't resist sharing some of the best with you.

How do you do it all?

> By far, time is my most valuable commodity. So when I say "yes" to any opportunity, I have to ask myself, "Am I going to pour something valuable into another person's life or is the opportunity going to pour something valuable into mine?" Over time I had to grow both my mental and leadership muscles so that I gained the needed capacity for this season. The person I was 25 years ago would have never been able to handle everything that I can handle now, nor could she be as clear about her priorities.

What do you look for in an emerging or up-and-coming leader?

> There is a lot of talent out there. It goes without saying, you desire to hire people that are talented. It is the one that is both talented and tenacious who catches my eye. The other thing I watch for is a keen sense of observation and curiosity. Some people are very observant, asking questions in order to solve and come up with alternative solutions. I also watch for the fruit of the Spirit in the life of another. When I see it, I know their character is ready for more growth.

How do you help someone develop their potential?

I like to share leadership development with others. Rather than trying to be the single voice or coach myself, I like to connect growing leaders to one or two people that I think could be valuable in helping them be ready for the next step in their journey. It's up to them to make the most of that opportunity.

It is a leadership tragedy when you operate from a place of undeveloped potential. You not only limit your own reach, impact, and influence, but you also stunt the growth and leadership development of the other leaders around you.

You matter more than you think. Therefore, you must take responsibility for your own personal and professional development. You have to grow in introspection first, learning to identify and address your interior motives, emotions and beliefs. You have to allow time and pain to buff the sharp edges of your character and sharpen the vision of your heart. At the same time, you also look outward, becoming increasingly aware of how your emotions and expectations are affecting others around you.

secret #9
LEADERS LOVE

Talking the language of love at work might be a little awkward. Frankly, in most environments talk of love might even be perceived as manipulative, embarrassing or even illegal. I'm not suggesting you talk about love. I'm suggesting you actually love.

> BUT THE *fruit* OF THE SPIRIT IS *love*, JOY, *peace*, FORBEARANCE, *kindness*, GOODNESS, *faithfulness*, GENTLENESS AND *self-control*. AGAINST SUCH THINGS THERE IS NO LAW.
>
> GALATIANS 5:22-23

Love is not a matter of words, but a matter of actions. Talking about your care for someone will only go so far. But when you show up day after day seeking the best interest of others, your love language will impact them dramatically. When you speak by the fruit of the Spirit, your voice echoes. Love—with and without words—is a universal language that bypasses cultural barriers, racial differences, gender biases, language challenges and even religious preferences. It is capable of breaking down walls, healing wounds, and giving power to all who need it.

Do you know an emotionally healthy love-leader? It's not really difficult to spot them. They stand out like lights in the midst of darkness. "The mark of a good leader is loyal followers; leadership is nothing without a following" (Proverbs 14:28 MSG). First of all, they generally have a loyal following because people are drawn to the grace that marks their lives.

Secondly, they are peaceful, approachable, and wise. They love well. They know themselves and accept themselves; therefore, they can know and accept others. "Love and truth form a good leader; sound leadership is founded on loving integrity" Proverbs 20:28 (MSG).

Jesus was and is a healthy love-leader. Consider these truths about Him:

- **JESUS KNEW (KNOWLEDGE) HIS PURPOSE AND DESTINY.**
  I don't mean to put down knowledge or try to diminish its power. Proverbs says, "Fear of the Lord is the foundation of wisdom. Knowledge of the Holy One results in good judgment" (Proverbs 9:10 NLT).

- **JESUS WAS ALWAYS MOVED BY COMPASSION (LOVE).**
  His miracles were always preceded by compassion. Take a moment and scan the Gospels looking for His motivation. You'll find love at the root of all His actions.

- **JESUS LOVED PEOPLE AND WAS A NATURAL TEAM BUILDER.**
  He did nothing in isolation except pray to the Father. He was constantly inviting others to come close and follow Him.

- **JESUS WAS AN EMPOWERING LEADER.**
  Following just three-years of public ministry Jesus left behind a team of leaders who rocked the ancient world, established the local church, and are still empowering us today through their legacy.

I want to share a story of how love can impact the life of an emerging leader. Wendy Moreland always stood out to me because she was so faith-filled and kind. She taught, prayed and encouraged with power and authority. Yet she was and is humble by nature. I had no idea that Wendy had been shaped by a grace-giving mentor who loved well. Her story reveals how much we need and are helped by love.

> In my late teens or early twenties, Margo was the first pastor's wife and women's pastor that saw something in me that I didn't see in myself. She spoke life over me, told me directly the gifts she saw in me, and encouraged me to believe the Word at face value.
>
> I'll never forget one day we were going to the mall in Shreveport, and she said, "Pastor Bill (her husband) said that he's never seen anyone with as much favor on their life as you!" My first thought was, "They love me enough to talk about me to each other privately." And the second thought was, "I'LL TAKE THAT COMPLIMENT!" She taught me that when you see something positive, you SHARE IT!

Wendy learned such a valuable lesson from her mentor who operated in love by speaking life over Wendy and calling out her gifts. I asked Wendy what advice she would want to share with you about how you can demonstrate loving leadership to another person.

> It's hard to grow while hiding in your closet. So look for private ways to serve and encourage others. Bake a cake, cook a meal, write a letter, or offer to watch someone's child. As you step out to serve, God will build your confidence. Stay in the Word and pray in the Spirit asking for boldness to be prepared in and out of season. Most importantly, practice the fruit of the Spirit, loving others as you go.

We all flourish under the influence of an authentic and loving leader who is easy to access and willing to share. Amber Colberg gives a beautiful summary of a grace-giving leader—one that is full of love.

Grace-giving leaders are gentle and wise with their words, recognizing and remembering their deep need for the Holy Spirit to guide them and lead them. They see the treasure inside of you, help you dust it off and breathe life into it. A loving leader selflessly encourages and supports you.

Maybe all this talk of love leaves you wondering how it relates to the reality of your leadership challenge. Well, let me share some secular evidence to reinforce these claims.

I'm guessing that you have spent quite a bit of time, money, energy and resources on your education. In addition to years of schooling, technology has given us the potential to become the most informed generation ever. We are living in the Information Age. For decades we have looked to intelligence and education as the best indicators of potential success.

We even developed a test to help us rank ourselves in terms of our innate intellectual capacity. You have heard of the IQ test that measures one's intelligence or Intelligence Quotient. It is generally accepted that this measure is a set value that changes little during one's lifetime. That is why we spend a large amount of time, money and talent on maximizing intelligence. It takes much effort to increase its potential. No matter how smart you are, intelligence without common sense or empathy creates relational disconnection which makes it more difficult to lead. When we view intelligence as the gage of potential, we pivot between pride and insecurity—between confidence and fear. High intelligence is not a reliable indicator of potential leadership success.

On the other hand, your EQ (Emotional Quotient) value is highly indicative of potential leadership success. EQ is defined as the innate ability (that is grace/power) to feel, use, communicate, recognize, remember, learn from, manage, and understand emotions—ours and others. It also measures our ability to act in a positive and empathetic way for the good of the team or the wider enterprise. People who score well in an EQ evaluation tend to be able to connect and respond to others with grace.

Everybody knows a story of a highly intelligent, very skilled person who was promoted into a new leadership role, only to fail. On the other hand, we've all heard about someone who was steady and dependable—but not necessarily extraordinary—who was promoted into a similar position and knocked it out of the park.

Daniel Goleman, author of *Emotional Intelligence: Why It Can Matter More Than IQ,* discovered nearly 90% of the difference between average leaders and star performers in senior leadership roles is attributable to emotional intelligence. He defines emotional intelligence as self-awareness and impulse control, persistence, zeal and self-motivation, empathy, and social deftness. He says, "These qualities mark people who excel in life, whose relationships flourish, who are stars in the workplace."

EQ is remarkably similar to spiritual maturity and Godly wisdom. As you emotionally mature, the quality of your relationships improves and your leadership skills grow more impactful. It is a life-long process that leaves your character marked by the master emotion of love. It is evident in the way you relate with others, the way you speak to them or about them, the respect you demonstrate, and the confidence you walk in.

People who score high in the EQ evaluation have learned to master their own emotions while dispensing a tremendous amount of love, joy, peace, patience, kindness, goodness, and self-control to others

(See Galatians 5 for more about the fruits of the Spirit). Therefore, they continually grow in healthy leadership, vital relationships, and their ability to lead others. With awareness and intention, you can focus on an area of emotional weakness, and by grace experience great mastery.

There is a groundswell of research showing that healthy leadership depends more upon the emotional health (EQ) of the leader than on their intellect (IQ). This only confirms what 1 Corinthians 8:1 says, "But knowledge puffs up while love builds up."

Grace and love rest on the EQ side of the equation. Consider the following verses:

> GO AFTER A *life* OF *love* AS IF YOUR LIFE DEPENDED ON IT—BECAUSE IT DOES. GIVE YOURSELVES TO THE *gifts* GOD GIVES YOU.
> 1 CORINTHIANS 14:1 MSG).

> JESUS REPLIED: "'LOVE THE LORD YOUR GOD WITH *all* YOUR *heart* AND WITH *all* YOUR *soul* AND WITH *all* YOUR *mind*.' THIS IS THE FIRST AND *greatest* COMMANDMENT. AND THE SECOND IS LIKE IT: *love* YOUR *neighbor* AS YOURSELF.'"
> MATTHEW 22:37-39

> ABOVE ALL, *love* EACH OTHER *deeply*, BECAUSE LOVE *covers* OVER A MULTITUDE OF SINS.
>
> 1 PETER 4:8

> "A *new* COMMAND I GIVE YOU: *love* ONE ANOTHER. AS I HAVE *loved* YOU, SO YOU MUST LOVE ONE ANOTHER. BY *this* EVERYONE WILL *know* THAT YOU ARE MY DISCIPLES, IF YOU *love* ONE ANOTHER."
>
> JOHN 13:34-35

> AND NOW THESE THREE *remain*: FAITH, HOPE AND LOVE. BUT THE *greatest* OF THESE IS *love*.
>
> 1 CORINTHIANS 13:13

Wendy K. Walters shares about her experience in this area as she learned to truly listen well to those she leads. She understood the power of love through listening and empowering others to seek for the answers themselves.

The longer I walk as a leader, the less advice I give. I have a gift for seeing a full picture from just a few fragmented pieces of the puzzle. In my early days, I could barely wait for someone to take a breath before I jumped in to share my insight and help them. It got me a lot of "Wow! That's amazing!" responses, and these affirmations fed my ego as people sought me out for my "prophetic insight" and "wisdom beyond my years."

I have since learned that listening deeply is a more precious gift. Having healing conversations is to be valued above the monologue at all costs. I still see the big picture, but now, instead of jumping in with advice, I pause and ask questions. Then I listen to those answers, pause, and ask some more questions just like Jesus did. "But who do you say that I am?" "Do you want to get well?" "Do you believe?" "Why are you so afraid?"

If you ask enough questions, sooner or later, the person who has come to you for guidance finds out that the Holy Spirit inside of them has held the answer all along. By waiting and listening and probing, they'll arrive at the picture on their own. Then, it has more meaning to them. Then, it builds confidence; it bears the joy of discovery and rewards their investment in searching out the mystery. Instead of needing a guru, they learn to trust The Guide.

I still love to talk. I have a million ideas coursing through my grey matter at any given moment. But now, I am learning to reign in my enthusiasm for the big reveal and cultivate the joy of sharing clues for their treasure hunt. Now, whenever possible, I frame my counsel through questions that lead to discovery rather than points to ponder or action items.

Love leaders can spot the potential in others and naturally bring unity and value to people over projects. Why would you wait any longer? Begin now to intentionally demonstrate a love and respect for others through the manifestations of a grace-giving leader. Share your experiences, failures, fears and dreams. Listen well to their thoughts and needs. Encourage the development of their gifts and interests. Pray for them. Be kind, patient, steadfast, forgiving, selfless, generous, thoughtful, honest, wise, and caring. Grace-giving leadership—empowering leadership—is all pulled together by love.

PAUSE AND PONDER

It's difficult to overemphasize the importance of love in our relationships. Whether in the workplace, our homes, or our communities, love is the most powerful tool we have to encourage others. The more love we experience, the more love we have to give. An overflow of love is an indicator of a healthy leader.

- Do you consider yourself a healthy love-leader? If so, how do you handle your emotions in an effective and responsible way? What advice would you give to others who struggle in this area?

- Since emotional intelligence (EQ) and spiritual maturity are similar in development and impact, what steps can you take to increase your innate ability (grace/power) to act in a positive and empathetic way for the good of others when you are under stress?

- What characteristics of an emotionally intelligent leader (power, humility, wisdom, revelation) do you need to see increased in your life? The word of God is a powerful catalyst for spiritual development. What Scripture verse or promise will you meditate upon in order to stimulate your growth in this area?

secret #10
LEADERS MULTIPLY

Leaders can raise up followers, or they can raise up leaders. One approach adds, the other multiplies. Good leadership isn't about just advancing yourself; that's simple addition. It is about advancing with a team; that's multiplication. There is a great exchange that happens in servant-hearted leadership. You give grace and others receive it. Miracles begin to happen as each person in the process is empowered and the results of the labor are multiplied. That is why I believe so deeply in mentoring. Mentoring is multiplication.

Relationships are important, and developing leaders can be so much fun. Maybe that is why I love mentoring so much. Mentoring creates effective relationships that naturally help leaders move from addition to multiplication.

Leaders want to walk with someone who will mentor them. They are always scanning the horizon for people, resources or ideas that will help them. The most effective mentors draw upon the roles of coach, advisor and friend to show, find and release the secret treasure inside another person that is often overlooked or even despised. They will take advantage of every opportunity to learn by putting the emphasis on the possibilities

> A TRUE *mentor* WILL SPEAK INTO YOUR *core identity* AND UNDERSCORE HOW *valuable* YOU ARE

rather than the problems. And, of course, a true mentor will speak into another's core identity and help move them along in understanding how valuable they are.

You may be aware that a large number of start-up companies fail each year. According to an article entitled "Data Shows Mentors are Vital to Small Business Success" by Kabbage, a global financial services, technology and data platform serving small businesses, "The early years of any business is a crucial make or break period, and most small businesses agree mentors are vital to success." According to their survey of more than 200 American small business entrepreneurs, the advantage provided by having a mentor is real.

Here are some of their findings:

- 89% of surveyed entrepreneurs don't currently have a mentor but wish they did.
- 92% of small business leaders agree mentors have a direct impact on growth and the survival of their business.
- 22% of small business leaders had a mentor when they started their business. Another 17% indicated they had some type of advisors. That means 63% of startups did not pursue professional guidance at the onset of their business.[1]

---

1. *Mentors are Vital to Success,* Kabbage. https://www.kabbage.com/resource-center/grow/data-shows-mentors-are-vital-to-small-business-success.

- These statistics clearly highlight the value of finding and enjoying the wisdom of a leader you trust. They should also confirm how important your leadership might be to someone else. We need mentors, and we need to mentor.

Here are a couple of simple steps to help you move from addition to multiplication, from developing yourself to developing others.

- BEGIN BY IDENTIFYING THE EMERGING LEADERS ALREADY AROUND YOU.
  Watch for those who have a natural tendency to serve. Be careful to evaluate more than their experience. Look closely for signs of maturity in attitude and deed. Who shows initiative? Who is forward thinking? Who demonstrates strong relational skills? Who is a problem solver? Who is inspiring, mobilizing or growing in their emotional, spiritual and mental strengths?

- DETERMINE IN WHOM YOU ARE WILLING TO INVEST.
  I can mentor and encourage many people at one time via teaching, writing or video broadcasting. That's good stewardship of my purpose. But to go beyond general mentoring to real leadership development requires a willingness on my part to share of my personal time, experience and resources. Because my most impactful leadership development happens face to face in small groups or personal settings, I am selective about who I am able to develop at this level. To help me determine who is ready for this type of encouragement I ask myself these three questions:

- **CAN THEY LEAD THEMSELVES?**

  The person who lacks self-leadership or self-awareness is not ready for the type of responsibility and empowerment I hope to share.

- **CAN THEY LEAD WITH ANOTHER?**

  Co-leading or partnering with another is a life skill that is developed over time and with growing maturity. If they can give and take in the leadership role, I know I have someone who is ready for more.

- **CAN THEY LEAD A TEAM?**

  Experience in leading a small group or team of people is excellent preparation for learning how to identify and develop other leaders.

- **SHARE POWER**

  How did you learn to lead? I learned to lead because at many points along my journey someone saw my potential and trusted me with responsibilities and experiences I had never had before. Trusting in another who is yet unproven takes greater grace and courage than giving responsibility to someone who has already demonstrated competency. This is where "the rubber meets the road" on your own journey to becoming an empowering leader. Are you ready to invest, risk and share in the rewards and the cost of leadership?

I asked several of my friends to share their best tips on how to personally identify, encourage or lead another emerging leader within one's own realm of influence. Here is what they said:

- I first ask God to highlight others to me then to place me in situations that will allow me to see what He's doing and how to partner with Him. This approach always seems to open a door to start a conversation. It allows me to see potential in others, and I spend time getting to know them first before anything else (Rhonda Love).

- I believe that every person has leadership potential, but it is those who choose to submit to someone in authority that seem to fulfill it. I love to see individuals who are teachable. Those who are willing to learn and submit to someone who is further down the road than they are always seem to be the best mentees. I love to encourage and find the unique gifts placed in each individual, especially when leading. So many people do not see their potential; it just requires some cultivation (Dr. Cassie Reid).

- I most often feel that people need a leader who will allow them to share what they are hearing the Lord impart to them and then affirm that they do, in fact, hear God. A number of years ago the Lord gave me the acronym T.E.A.C.H. This stands for: To Encourage, Activate, Cultivate, Hearing...God. Emerging leaders were invited to be part of a home growth group that I facilitated and hosted allowing a different woman each week to take the entire 2 hours and lead however she wanted. Permission fueled with affirmation is a powerful statement to an emerging leader. There is a partnership involved in launching out leaders. Honoring each other's giftings and anointings and being willing to have the Lord advance someone ahead of you, are a grace Jesus desires us all to walk in (Kristin Paschke).

- When it comes to identifying an emerging leader, I look for someone who is humble, willing to learn, and faithful. It's having a teachable spirit that really stands out to me. When you pair that with someone who consistently shows up and is trustworthy, that is the type of person I want to invest in. They may not be the loudest person in the room, but their character speaks loudly for them. I encourage emerging leaders by finding out what makes them tick, what gets them excited, and then stir that pot. It's about finding out what may seem a little scary to them and then providing safe spaces for them to try, learn and grow. When they might not be able to see their potential and giftings, I love to call those things out of them and show them that they have someone in their corner cheering them on to succeed (Emily Miller).

- To identify a leader, I pay attention to people's communication. Are they timid or do they speak up? When speaking, do they dominate, or do they leave room for others' input? Do they speak with compassion or with an authoritarian attitude? There is a balance of speaking up and staying quiet in leading so that the leader clearly conveys their vision while also involving others to join them in carrying it out. To encourage, I use words to point out to that person specific giftings and abilities I see within them. Calling out strengths builds confidence in identity and ability (Courtney Cohen).

A mentor is important for you. But if you stop at that point, you are only adding to yourself. At some point, you will become a mentor, and when that happens, you will begin to multiply. Proximity is often a primary needed ingredient to become a mentor. You don't have to be older in age. You just have to be a few steps ahead of the person you are mentoring. Our teenagers can mentor our pre-teens. Our young women can influence significantly the generation right behind them. As we age, we even look for someone who has walked through a similar journey or whose life is producing a fruit we desire.

So who is already within your circle of relationships that is teachable, eager for wisdom, and open to relationship? That's the girl you should begin mentoring.

PAUSE AND PONDER

One of the most effective ways to practice empowering leadership is through the formation of small groups. Consider gathering a community of individuals you want to invest in and draw them together around a common interest or topic. Then be intentional to give of yourself freely. At the same time, invite those in the group to share in the responsibilities of serving. You will soon recognize those who are ready to lead and those who are ready for the greater responsibility of leading leaders.

- How do you know when it's time to entrust another leader with a greater measure of responsibility?

- What characteristics do you look for in emerging leaders? What do these characteristics indicate to you about their potential success?
- What characteristics do you look for in a leader of leaders? How is this different than identifying an emerging leader?

> I GIVE *grace* BECAUSE I SO DESPERATELY *need* IT.
>
> —LYSA TERKEURST

chapter six

MAKE IT PERSONAL

I want to share one final story of my own leadership journey. This story is still unfolding, but I hope one day it will be a testimony of how grace-giving leadership leaves a legacy of strength and courage for others to receive. I've saved this story for last because it is intimate, close to my heart, and still evolving. Like most good stories it was birthed in the midst of weakness and fear.

I've shared a lot about my failings, weaknesses and even terrible mistakes along the way to becoming a better leader, but I am hesitant to share my positive outcomes and label them as successful. I don't really know if any of us can evaluate our own success or even really understand our legacy. I try to remember that when I get to see Jesus face to face, He won't be talking to me about writing a book or hosting a mega-event. He will talk with me about how my life impacted people for His glory and their good.

I agree with the Apostle Paul who wrote, "What matters most to me is to finish what God started: the job the Master Jesus gave me of letting everyone I meet know all about this incredibly extravagant generosity of God" (Acts 20:24 MSG).

> **Journal Entry: Tuesday, October 13, 2015**
>
> My husband so sweetly told me this week that he was proud of me, and that I was brave and strong. I so want to be brave and strong, but the truth is I mostly just feel weak and afraid. Cancer is a disease that dogs you. It just nips at your heels, threatens your peace and has a nasty habit of camouflaging itself for long seasons and suddenly reappearing in new locations with new vengeance. Even when you are cancer free, it whispers around the corners of your ears and reminds you that you are weak.

It was the fall of 2015 when I was diagnosed with a return of breast cancer. I had been cancer free for six years. For a few weeks, I knew something was wrong, but despite an onslaught of testing, we couldn't find the problem. By the time we discovered the recurrence, I had a metastasis in both my brain and my liver.

Maybe you can relate to the devastation I experienced. There are many moments that sideswipe our plans and significantly impact our future. Often these things are beyond our control. They don't just touch us; they touch our families, friends and greater community. This kind of pain comes to us and produces both weakness and fear.

Most of us spend our lives trying to hide, overcome or even deny our weakness and fears, believing that our cracks and imperfections disqualify us from a life of influence and love. It never really crosses our mind that our weakness and fear are the places of hidden treasure from which courage and strength will spring forth.

I had no idea how God might use that experience to make me brave and strong, but I can assure you, He did. He began by giving me such an intimate sense of His presence that I felt more peace than fear, more hope than despair. Without any effort on my part, without a conscious decision to believe, without any sign of hope or a word of prophecy, He came and drove out fear. According to the apostle John, there is only one force in all the universe powerful enough to drive out fear, and that is God's perfect love.

> THERE IS *no* FEAR IN *love*. BUT *perfect* LOVE DRIVES OUT FEAR, BECAUSE FEAR HAS TO DO WITH PUNISHMENT. THE ONE WHO FEARS IS NOT *made perfect* IN LOVE.
> 1 JOHN 4:18

During that season, I was studying the leadership journey of Joshua, and I learned that when God told Joshua to take courage (nine times in the first chapter of Joshua alone) it wasn't because Joshua was a big chicken who needed to be coerced into obeying. It was because true courage requires obedience in the face of great fear. It was and is a fearsome thing to trust God enough to simply wait on His grace when you are so vulnerable or broken.

"Be still before the Lord; wait patiently for Him and entrust yourself to Him; Do not fret (whine, agonize) because of him who prospers in his way *(like cancer, fear, or worry)*, Because of the man who carries out wicked schemes" (Psalm 37:7 AMP, second parenthetical and italicized words added).

And, I learned something about the strength He gives. No one ever told me that you can be completely, totally unable to do one thing for yourself or others—and yet, in that moment—find there is still some thin strand of strength that just won't let go. His grace produces tenacity in the heart of the believer. Paul heard the Lord say:

> "MY *grace* IS *sufficient* FOR YOU, FOR MY *power* IS MADE *perfect* IN WEAKNESS."

Paul's response was, "Therefore I will boast all the more gladly about my weaknesses, so that Christ's power may rest on me" (2 Corinthians 12:9).

This intimate experience of the presence of the Holy Spirit at my greatest need—overriding and propelling me through such a difficult season of war—caused me to finally develop the greater fruits of the spirit: love, joy and peace. Grace began to pour through my struggle and produce something beautiful.

I began to share more about my experience on a blog called Brave Strong Girl. Eventually, it has become a place of community where others are being encouraged to boldly overcome fear and weakness through faith-based mentorship, connection, collaboration and resources. There I discovered that others could connect and be encouraged through my weakness. I became less concerned about being so strong and more focused on Christ's power resting in me. Even this book, the other resources and mentoring relationships offered as a part of the community, were birthed out of this season of trusting God when all else seemed impossible.

At Brave Strong Girl, we believe that every woman is a warrior who has the ability to make a difference in the lives of others. A true warrior's strength comes not from her tools, experiences or even her imagination. Rather, it rises from a divine call, a sense of purpose, and a holy hope that her experiences, pain and trials can be used to change her world and the worlds of those around her. She is empowered, not by her own strength or courage, but by a constant dependence upon the Holy Spirit who presses her to rise above her fear and weakness. She is influential and anointed—brave and strong.

That's you—brave and strong. I hope when you finish this portion of your leadership development journey, you will consider bringing your gifts and your needs to the Brave Strong Girl community where you are needed and loved.

It has been more than a decade since my original diagnosis and almost five years since the recurrence. Today, I have no evidence of cancer in my body, yet I continue preventative care in order to sustain my healing. In the future, I may battle another manifestation. It reminds me that weak and afraid is a posture God can move through. Some would say my life is miraculous. I think it's a testimony. My life is a testimony to the grace of God working deeply inside the heart (and body) of a woman overwhelmed by grace.

If you've gotten this far in the journey with me, I know you are both powerful and courageous too. You want to let your light shine. You are passionate about becoming a grace-giving leader. You have counted the cost and considered the consequences of an empowering lifestyle, and you are willing to freely share what has been freely given to you.

I know how hard it is to get to this place, and I do not take lightly whatever God might have planned for your life. But, let me remind you that the reward for this courageous journey is life changing for you and for those you lead. So much is at stake—not only your future—but the future of the people you are called to love and serve. It doesn't get much more personal than this.

So now let the deeper work begin—the work of letting go of your fear so that you are free to liberate others. Embrace what feels weak or broken as a place where God's love can shine through you and touch others. This transformation you seek will not happen by accident. You must take specific and intentional steps to deepen and accelerate your own leadership journey in order to have the transformational experience that will change lives.

Working through this study material and learning how to authentically care about empowering others has been your first step. Now as you advance into the next level of love, I am offering you my ten best tips for becoming a grace-giving leader.

---

1. GO AHEAD AND *lead*.

Leaders lead. Leadership inherently includes a responsibility to effectively steward the people, resources and opportunities set before you. So, don't let leadership paralysis overtake you.

Whether you have a formal position of leadership or you are simply cultivating a leadership lifestyle, begin with what you have and where you are.

Leadership development is a life-long process forged in the fire of actually leading. Becoming an empowering leader is not just about communication, talking, or listening; it's actually about your attitude, character, and what you do.

Go ahead and ask God for the grace you need right where you are. Then boldly take the first step. Just do something. Be compelled to bite the bullet and begin. Repeat this daily and you will find yourself leading with grace. Set forth and model a leadership style that is worthy of emulating and inspires others to grow.

2. ASSUME PEOPLE ARE *capable*.

You won't know the potential in people until you begin to believe that potential exists within them and that they are capable of more. People tend to rise to our expectations. So, what are you expecting? Do you have a fundamental faith in people or a fundamental distrust?

When you assume that people are capable, you will entrust them with assignments and responsibilities that are on the edge of their experience. This is how you find treasure in people. You believe in their potential, not just in their track record. If you believe your team members desire to be successful and to contribute effectively to the mission, then demonstrate that belief by expressing confidence in their abilities. (If you don't believe these things, then why are they on your team?)

This courageous and grace-giving stance may cause you some difficulties. The truth is, almost everything we do is done poorly when we first start doing it. That's how we learn. You will have to allow room for failure, mistakes, and learning curves. You may have to step in and help your team members accomplish the task or cross the finish line. Regardless of the additional support or encouragement they require, you will reap the benefit of a fast-developing leadership lifestyle that will be impactful.

3. CAST *vision*.

It is so important to learn to cast vision to your team. Teams, consumers, and even communities are more motivated by the why of your mission than by the how. Don't expect people to stay excited about the mission if you aren't excited about the mission.

Casting vision not only defines the "win," but also explains what is expected or required of the team. Don't just answer the question, "What's the goal?" Go ahead and answer the unspoken question of their heart, "Is what I am doing making a difference?"

Work hard on improving your communication skills so that vision casting becomes an inherent part of your leadership style. Learn to make your words "salty"—seasoned with respect and confidence. Lay a table before others that is appealing and focuses on the potential impact of an empowered team.

4. **TAKE MORE *risks*.**

    Risk-taking yields great rewards. Not only should you take more risks but consider giving others an opportunity to do the same. Risk-taking for the thrill of the ride is stupid, but risk-taking in order to break through barriers or stimulate creativity will always garner excitement and reveal hidden treasure in people. It's true you might fall short more often, but in the long-term you will advance further.

    Begin elementary risk-taking by giving others more permission to draw their own conclusions, determine their own applications, and steward their own portion of the work. Clearly define the measurable objectives but leave room for the strategy and tactics. If everyone has to do everything just like you, then you've limited the entire team's capacity and destroyed creative potential within others.

    Consider creating meaningful and collaborative learning experiences that will accelerate the preparation required to release others into greater authority. When they need help, begin by asking questions that give them a chance to verbally process and then help them reach solutions that are viable. Don't provide the answer for them. If you do, they will learn that coming up with a solution is not something you expect of them. You might think you are helping, but actually you will train them in learned helplessness.

5. ALLOW FOR AND *forgive* FAILURE.

When you empower and encourage people to be creative problem solvers and risk-takers, you would be wise to also communicate they have permission to fail and try again. Failure is not the end; failure is only an opportunity to begin again. If you allow others the freedom to make mistakes and recover, then they will extend the same grace to you.

Forgive quickly and don't hold a grudge. Keep your focus on how they can improve and how you can help. Remember my story about the boss who gave me no grace? When your team has made a mistake or experienced a failure, they are already reprimanding themselves, looking for someone else to blame, or running from the consequences. You can preempt this negative cycle by talking about failure in advance. Exposing the "elephant in the room" will reduce fear and increase courage.

Take time to debrief all along the way so that you can strategize adjustments for the future and encourage others to try again. Small failures lead to big breakthroughs. Giant failures lead to huge consequences and loss of empowerment.

6. PROVIDE *resources* AND *encouragement*.

Give people as many tools, training, and resources as you can in order to equip them for their responsibilities. Sometimes we approach a mission with an attitude of lack or stinginess expecting others to "produce more bricks with less straw" (Exodus 5:7). Turn that approach around and generously resource your team for maximum effectiveness.

Don't withhold what you have or what they need to facilitate the vision. This is an example of giving people responsibility without authority. It's a set up for failure and nobody will win. You might feel secure in the beginning but eventually you will realize that you are holding others back from success.

Become known for your generosity. Be the first to share your resources and encouragement. Think creatively with your team about how to overcome shortages of time, resources, or solutions. Keep your door open and make your team feel welcome when they approach you with questions. Connect and give generously, and you will reap the rewards.

7. BUILD *community*.

All of us have a desire to be a part of something bigger than ourselves. We want our life to have meaning and purpose. We don't just work for a paycheck. People work best when they feel a part of a community where everyone is valued and are able to contribute toward something meaningful. People will actually work for less reward if they are working in a great community.

Do you want to accomplish big goals? You'll need a lot of human resources. You will need to make time for the people on your team a high priority. If the goals are big, you will need to slow down. It's true that you can go fast and take only a few people along, or you can slow down and take thousands. If you need greater unity, more contribution, or simply a better working environment, concentrate on how to authentically connect with people.

Whether you are building a product, selling a service, or leading a group, you can invite others into your circle of influence. Caring about other people is more important than caring about what they can do for you or with you.

8. PRIORITIZE *people* OVER RESULTS.

Our American economy is so profit-driven that it is common to work in environments where the leadership values results over people. This is a short-term and highly expensive method of reaching a goal. You will burn through staff, gain a poor reputation, and often find yourself out of business. When results trump people, you are at great risk of damaging others and destroying your business.

Profitability is an important goal and one I embrace. But, when you only care about what people can do for you, employees will soon develop a slave mindset. They may do the work, but they will do it without enthusiasm or excellence. In addition, they will not apply themselves to new endeavors or creative solutions. They may function, but they will be disengaged. Good leaders and strong employees will not tolerate this attitude. They will leave and move on to better opportunities.

The number one way to tell people you care about them is to communicate that they are more important than the results they produce. When you legitimately care about the people on the mission with you, you will build empowering, creative, and loyal communities who function well and are profitably sustainable over time. Let building healthy relationships and an authentic community trump mere results every time.

9. BE *patient*.

    Make room in your leadership style to accept people where they are while encouraging them to move toward greater maturity. We all know people are naturally chaotic. All of us are moving from lost to found, and everyone needs more grace. We must learn to be patient while people are in the process of being transformed.

    It's what you do and how you respond when others need more grace that reveals your true self. Check your own character before withholding grace from another who is pushing your buttons, pressing the limits, or even downright making it hard for everyone. Sometimes grace will look like correction or even redirection, but it will never be cruel, impatient, or condescending.

    Patience is also required when you are empowering others to lead. It takes time, feedback, and experience to gain the confidence to lead with grace. This is not a one-stop shop where you encourage someone once and they catapult to success. This is a process of learning and growing. Your ability to give grace is directly related to the depth of your own patience.

10. TAKE TIME TO *celebrate*.

    Working together should be fun! One of the best ways to "bring the fun" is to celebrate milestones with one another. Celebration is a powerful tool too often neglected. We fail to stop and acknowledge positive change and simply rush to set the next milestone. This can result in serious discouragement for a goal-driven team.

Don't be the leader who points out problems without celebrating progress. Rather, consider creative ways to recognize and celebrate great results—both individual and team. Give away the credit for success to others. Find a way to commemorate important achievements and build reward into your recognition. I am amazed at how excited people get over a $10 gift card to the local coffee shop or how competitive they will become to win a pizza party. Don't forget or underestimate the power of regular affirmation and words of encouragement.

Reward and celebrate hard work and consistent grace-giving leadership with advancement opportunities and proper compensation for outstanding team members. Recognition and reward should come in every form—from a simple shout out at a team meeting to a congratulations note tucked inside a well earned bonus check. Don't hold onto people resisting their advancement opportunities for the better of your team or your future. That's a pretty cruddy reason to hide the accomplishments or strengths of another person, and it totally lacks grace. If you can't promote or bonus an individual, remember that public and private recognition for a job well done inspires the whole team to achieve with excellence and builds tremendous loyalty.

You will lead many times in your life whether through your marketplace responsibilities, your spiritual assignments, or your friends and family relationships. Sometimes a leadership responsibility will catch you by surprise. Perhaps even now you are in a moment where you are not certain what to do or how to proceed. Congratulations! You are in a moment of great grace, and you have an opportunity to humbly trust God and obey.

Kristin Lemus is so good at helping all of us understand how God works and what He expects.

> God doesn't call you because you are perfect, know all you need to know or have figured out how to do everything right the first time. God calls you because you are willing to say, "Yes," no matter what. He faithfully teaches you what you need to know along the way. You get to be imperfect and make mistakes. You even get to give up and start again. If you feel inadequate for the task ahead, you are not alone. Most of us do. Those who see their dreams realized are the ones who keep getting back up when they make mistakes and who keep trusting that God knows what He is doing with their dreams.

Maybe you are asking where do I go from here? Next steps are always so helpful for me, so I want to give you one final boost to help you reach your highest leadership potential. Here are some specific next steps and some final advice for you.

- **MAKE A QUALITY *decision* TO BECOME AN EMPOWERING, GRACE-GIVING LEADER.**

    Everything you do begins with a decision to do it. Have you really made a decision to become an empowering, grace-giving leader? Your will is important. God will not force you to become a leader. But if you want to be, then ask God for what you really need—more grace (Secret #1 – Grace Empowers). Starting the journey by going to God for your own empowerment will change your life and the impact of your leadership.

- *embrace* WHO YOU ARE.

    Understanding who you are and embracing what you discover is an amazing part of the leadership journey. The more you appreciate your own personality and gifts, the more grateful and free you will be to share with others. In my book *Women at War*, I wrote about my own journey of discovering how to really love who I am and how God made me. The journey changed my life and I wanted to share it with others (Secret #4 Grace Received Empowers You). It will be difficult to reach your full potential as a leader if you struggle with wounds, fears or lies. You need a touch of God's healing grace to overcome long-standing pain, as well as to embrace an empowering future.

- THINK ABOUT *who* YOU ARE CALLED TO *lead*.

    Begin figuring this out by simply looking around your immediate sphere of influence and asking yourself, "Who can I serve?" There you go; that's your current leadership responsibility. Maybe your current sphere is not so exciting and not really what you were dreaming about (Secret #7 – Leadership is Not About You). Nevertheless, begin right where you are. Trust God to fill in the gap between here and now and what you hope for in the future. Ask anyone you see as a successful leader, and they will confirm this: "Begin with what's in your hands right now." Remember that people are God's greatest treasure, and He takes their care and development very seriously (Secret #8 – Leadership is Always About Others). Be careful that you never despise those you are serving.

- **EVALUATE YOUR CURRENT LEADERSHIP *health*.**

    In the addendum you will find a quiz called Are You a Grace-Giving Leader? This tool will help you better understand your current leadership health. Take the test. Then ask one or two people who are close to you and who will be honest to also take the test. Then compare and contrast your results. This simple exercise will help reveal your blind spots and determine the most critical changes you can make right away to improve your health and your impact on others. It will also highlight where you are already an exceptional grace-giving leader.

- ***Begin* WHERE YOU ARE.**

    Dream big but begin right where you are. Now that you understand that leadership has little to do with waiting on someone else to call out your gifts, you can look around and serve with passion right where you are. I recommend you begin with love (Secret #9: Leaders Love). Love others fearlessly and have their back. No one can resist pure love, and no one needs permission to love. If you will simply serve faithfully with whatever is in your hands, you will soon see and feel the impact and influence of love leadership on others (Secret #5: Grace Given Empowers Others).

- **KEEP *good* COMPANY.**

    Be intentional to surround yourself with people who share your values, have experience in your current life season, and are hopeful. You become like the company you keep. Take a moment to evaluate your current community of friends and co-workers. How are they influencing you for the good? Do you need to make some changes (Secret #6: Grace Withheld Disempowers)?

- **REACH OUT AND *connect*.**

    Find some trailblazers and reach out to them. Identify some "pioneers" in your field of interest who demonstrate an unshakeable confidence in their call and who have stopped putting limitations on themselves or others. Then, don't waste time (Secret #2: Grace Connects). Be brave and initiate some new relationships. You could arrange a meeting, send a note or email, and respond to their blogs or written materials. Be prepared to ask questions and to glean specific advice. The responsibility to make the connection worthwhile rests on you (Secret #3: Grace Matures). Don't forget that books are also a powerful way to glean from those who have lived a life that inspires you.

- **GIVE *grace* AWAY.**

    Practice intentionally responding with grace to those around you. Grace is not just about being kind when someone messes up. That's the elementary version. Fully developed grace is about having the heart of God for others. It's about seeing something special in them and carefully nurturing it to development. It's about saving someone from a major mistake, withholding your judgment when you don't understand, and reaching out to those who isolate or are insecure. It's about helping a potential leader reign in their passion and develop their character before launching into responsibilities greater than they are ready to bear. Open doors for their gifts, share from your wealth of wisdom, be kind to everyone you meet, and celebrate when those who follow become those who lead (Secret #10: Leaders Multiply).

I hope this journey has been very personal, and that it has encouraged you to be the leader God designed you to be. It's no accident that you have the passion, drive, and willingness to be a leader. God planted those desires in you so that you would be uniquely equipped to do whatever you are doing right now! I echo this encouragement:

> EMBRACE THE *season* YOU ARE IN.
> DON'T GIVE UP. DON'T BACK OFF.
> YOU ARE DOING A *great* WORK.
> YOU ARE DOING WHAT GOD
> IS *calling* YOU TO DO.
>
> —CRAIG GROESCHEL

Yes, you are leading right now in a God-given, potentially grace-filled assignment. Everything you've learned, everything you've experienced, and everything you are is leading toward greater grace in the future.

When I look back over my life, I can see the puzzle pieces coming together. I can identify God's hand on my life providing me with experiences that have equipped me to serve as a pastor and leader today. I have benefited from an immense amount of grace and patience from many leaders and, of course, from God.

It's thrilling to think about the opportunities now awaiting you. When I look around and note the character of the women God is using all around the world, I can hardly keep my feet on the ground. You are well on your way to becoming a grace-giving leader. You are better, smarter, and stronger than you know. You can do and be anything God asks. And why not? Who wouldn't want to aspire to change the world for the better, leave a legacy of grace for those who follow, and feel the pleasure of God as they serve?

No matter what life brings, you can rest in God's grace. Go ahead and take that weight off your shoulders. Instead, put on the garment of a servant. You are the steward; you are not the owner. You are responsible for being faithful, but God is responsible for the outcome.

So, get going. Now is the time to take the first step—and then the next. Before you know it, you will be well on your way to experiencing new adventures.

I am cheering you on!

GRACE ISN'T A LITTLE *prayer* YOU CHANT BEFORE RECEIVING A MEAL. IT'S A *way* TO *live*. THE LAW TELLS ME HOW *crooked* I AM. GRACE COMES ALONG AND *straightens* ME OUT.

—D.L. MOODY

review

GRACE-GIVING LEADERSHIP SECRETS

secret #1
GRACE EMPOWERS

secret #2
GRACE CONNECTS

secret #3
GRACE MATURES

secret #4
GRACE RECEIVED EMPOWERS YOU

secret #5
GRACE GIVEN EMPOWERS OTHERS

secret #6
GRACE WITHHELD DISEMPOWERS

secret #7
LEADERSHIP IS NOT ABOUT YOU

secret #8
LEADERSHIP IS ALWAYS ABOUT OTHERS

secret #9
LEADERS LOVE

secret #10
LEADERS MULTIPLY

appendix

ARE YOU A GRACE-GIVING LEADER?

Consider each statement below as it applies to you and your leadership skills. When you finish the assessment, ask a close friend or someone on your team to take it with you in mind. Then compare your results. You are not rating your intentions "How I hope to lead" but rather your actual behavior "How am I leading?"

I seek to understand and know myself.	True/False
I seek to understand and know others.	True/False
I ask others for feedback on my behaviors.	True/False
I am approachable.	True/False

I am a team player and value "us" more than "me."	True/False
I am flexible and can negotiate for a win/win solution.	True/False
I don't hold grudges, and I extend forgiveness easily.	True/False
I am not defensive when approached by others.	True/False
I am able to resolve conflict in a healthy way.	True/False
I use empathy and compassion to avoid hurting others.	True/False
I am open to dialogue with those who disagree with me.	True/False
I live with self-confidence, but I am not arrogant.	True/False
I can see potential in others.	True/False
I enjoy helping others develop their gifts and interest.	True/False
I seek to identify the strengths and passions in others.	True/False
I enjoy teamwork.	True/False
I am able to entrust responsibility to others with ease.	True/False
I respond to mistakes and failures of others with grace.	True/False

WHAT DID YOU LEARN ABOUT YOURSELF?

Self-awareness is a necessary tool for a leader who wants to empower others. Your goal is to become aware of your emotions and how they are affecting your leadership.

_____
_____
_____
_____
_____

IS THERE AN AREA YOU WANT TO FOCUS UPON FOR IMPROVEMENT?

There may be some areas you identified that need improvement. Review your answers and look for trends. Determine one or two things you want to work on improving so that you can become a more empowering leader. Now is a great time to invite a coach/friend to take the assessment on your behalf and review your results.

_____
_____
_____
_____

DID YOU FIND SOME PLACES THAT YOU ARE ESPECIALLY STRONG?

Identifying your leadership strengths is exciting. Consider how you will take this information and empower others. List a few action steps you want to take to begin your journey.

_____

_____

_____

_____

_____

_____

_____

_____

grace-giving study guide

DISCUSSION QUESTIONS FOR LEADERS

chapter 1
LACED WITH GRACE

1. Share a little bit about your leadership journey to-date, and what you hope to learn about becoming a grace-giving leader.

2. What type of management style do you prefer? Do you like a team approach? Or are you more of a work alone kind of person? Do you need encouragement? Clear guidelines? More freedom? Take the time to consider the optimal environment for your best performance and share it with your team.

3. Would you consider yourself an eager leader or a reluctant leader? Explain.

4. Identify a leader or two who have impacted your life. Would you describe your experiences as mostly sweet or mostly bitter? Why?

5. Think of an empowering leader you love to follow. Now name at least three character traits of that person that stand out to you. Which of these traits do you see in yourself? Which traits do you want to develop?

6. Do you have some secrets of your own to becoming a grace-giving leader? Please list and share.

7. Name a woman or two from the Bible who have had the greatest mentoring impact on your life. What is it about their story or example that speaks to you?

8. Do you agree that the best reason for wanting to be a grace-giving leader is so that you "can help as many people as possible"? Why or why not?

9. Make a list of two or three leadership mistakes you've already experienced. Then share with someone—not only the mistakes, but also the lessons learned. Write them down and remember them.

10. What other investments are you committed to making in your leadership development? Will you identify a mentor? Will you work on developing a new skill? Will you overcome a fear or weakness? How will you use this experience to really grow?

chapter 2
GRACE TO WAIT

1. In this chapter, we talked about how God will use seasons of service, obscurity or waiting so that we might turn to Him for validation and your assignments. What season of waiting have you most recently experienced? What did you learn? How can you reevaluate what you might have experienced as a result of this chapter?

2. In what ways has God used a waiting season in your life to prepare you for a future assignment?

3. Do you agree with the statement, "Waiting is harder than doing"? Why or why not?

4. In Secret #1 (Grace Empowers), we learned that grace is the key to power. In what ways have you already been transformed by grace? Can you share a specific example?

5. What is the difference between grace and comparison? Is comparison a "cheap substitute" for grace? Are there any other counterfeits of grace that come to mind?

6. How easy or difficult is it for you to practice Secret #2 (Grace Connects)? Are there particular situations where you are successful at this skill? Are there moments when you struggle?

7. Name a time when you were able to make a connection with another person through a simple act of grace. What was the other person's response? How did it make you feel? What is your favorite act of humble care?

8. In this chapter, we list pretending, people pleasing, perfectionism and discontentment as signs of a lack of connection. Which of these symptoms do you experience most often? What can or will you do to overcome them?

9. In Secret #3 (Grace Matures) we learn that obedience produces noble character. Why do you think God requires noble character to exercise grace? What is your greatest character trait? Which traits are you still developing?

10. We identified some characteristics that often mark the life of an emotionally mature leader. Identify a leader who you feel reflects these characteristics. What is it about them that you admire or would want to emulate?

chapter 3
THE POWER TO CHANGE

1. In your own words, describe the difference between what grace is and what grace does.

2. Why is "simple elegance and refinement of movement" an important kind of grace to pursue? How does this type of grace impact your leadership potential?

3. In Secret #4 (Grace Received Empowers You) we learned that the Holy Spirit is the greatest grace-giver. How important is it to receive grace from the Holy Spirit before you strive to give grace to others?

4. On a simple scale of 1-10, how would you rate your ability to simply receive grace from the Lord? Please explain.

5. What do you need grace to accomplish? Maybe you need the power—the will and ability—to change your financial habits. You might have a marriage that needs attention. Maybe there is someone you've tried to forgive and simply haven't been able to do it. Perhaps you have a dream inside you that you can't seem to birth. What does God have to say about your need for power? Find a key promise in God's Word that relates to your need and meditate upon it.

6. In Secret #5 (Grace Given Empowers Others) I shared a personal story of how I was impacted by a leader who knew how to extend grace to me in a moment of weakness. Have you ever experienced this kind of grace? If so, how did it change you?

7. Do you have any concern about the possibility of giving people grace resulting in negative behavior or consequences? If so, why? How will you address this concern in yourself or others?

8. In Secret #6 (Grace Withheld Disempowers) we learned that both the withholding of trust and the threat of punishment are methods of controlling others that lack grace. Have you ever experienced this type of leadership? Have you ever led using these tools? What will you do differently in the future as a result of your experience?

9. It takes a grace-giving encounter to heal the damage caused by a grace-withholding experience. Can you identify one or two people in your own life that have been injured by a lack of grace? What could you do to help them heal and experience true grace?

10. The more grace you receive, the more it will spill over in your life to those around you. How can you intentionally splash some grace on someone else who needs healing, feels weak or even powerless? How might this change their lives? How might it change yours?

chapter 4
THE POWER TO INFLUENCE

1. What comes to mind when you think of leadership? Would you categorize your feelings about leadership as positive or negative? How do these things affect your life choices and leadership experiences?

2. Have you ever experienced a faulty foundation? How did you address the problem? What would you recommend to others with a similar issue? Can you identify a few cracks in your foundation today? What is causing them? How will you begin to repair the damage?

3. How important is it to you to become a restorative leader? Please explain.

4. In Secret #7 (Leadership Is Not About You) I highlighted some common myths that are often motivators in our leadership journey. Which of these myths have you struggled to overcome, and what advice would you give to an emerging leader that is struggling over the same issue?

5. Identify one or two leadership responsibilities you have had that were not labeled by a title or formal position. How did you exercise leadership? What did you learn about yourself in the process? How important are titles to you? Have they ever hindered your development?

6. Secret #8 (Leadership is Always About Others) puts a strong emphasis on the idea of servant leadership. Can you give an

example of a time when someone served you as a leader? How did that make you feel? How do you serve others?

7. "If you want to be a better leader, become a better follower." In what ways have you experienced this truth? How has your experience as a follower impacted your ability to lead?

8. "You won't be a great leader or part of an effective team if you have issues with authority." Do you agree or disagree with this statement? Which of your life experiences may have contributed to this viewpoint?

9. Name at least three teams of which you are a member. Now consider how you can more effectively partner with others on your team. List one or two specific steps you will make in the next month to improve your contribution (service) to the team.

10. So, we've talked about what leadership is (becoming a servant, being a follower, stewarding authority, embracing teamwork) and what it's not (not about genius, position, fame, or control). How is your growing understanding of true Biblical leadership impacting your thinking? Your plans? How you see others? Your definition of leadership?

chapter 5
THE POWER TO LEAD

1. As you evaluate your current leadership level ask yourself, "Who am I, and what do I represent?" What changes, if any, will you make as a result of your answer? (Taking the quiz Are You a Grace-Giving Leader included in the addendum is a good tool to help you self-evaluate.)

2. Insecurity is a root problem that many leaders struggle to overcome. If you were coaching an emerging leader around this issue, what advice would you give to them? Why?

3. In Secret #9 (Leaders Love), we touched on the idea of love as a critical factor in the development of spiritual maturity and Godly wisdom. How important do you feel love is to your ability to lead?

4. Have you ever considered that love might serve as a "jump start" to empowering others? In what ways could love give courage, acceptance, or more grace to those who feel uncertain? And how might this accelerate their growth?

5. Contrast and compare IQ with EQ. What is your most significant discovery? What investments have you made in either of these values? What will you do differently as you go forward?

6. Is there someone who has the authority and permission to speak into your life? If so, how has their mentorship impacted you? If not, what can you do to identify and connect with a potential leadership mentor?

7. Using the steps outlined in Secret #10 (Leaders Multiply), what actions do you plan to take to move from addition to multiplication?

8. Can you identify one or two emerging leaders in your current sphere of influence that you could help become more effective leaders by sharing your power? How could grace and love accelerate their leadership skills?

9. Do you want to become a leader of leaders? Why or why not? If so, what will you do to take more risk at your current leadership level?

10. In this chapter, several contributors shared their best tips for identifying, encouraging and leading emerging leaders. What was your favorite tip? Do you have some tips of your own? Please share.

chapter 6
MAKE IT PERSONAL

1. Have you ever experienced being brave and strong when you only felt weak and afraid? What was the most difficult part? What was the most supernatural part? What did you learn?

2. Have you ever experienced (or created) a leadership lid? How did you address the problem? What would you recommend to others?

3. What is the greatest personal challenge you have faced to date? Who helped you through that challenge, and what was the outcome? How can your new lens of grace help you process any residue or disappointment that might linger?

4. In this chapter, I shared 10 tips for becoming a grace-giving leader. Which of the 10 tips did you find most helpful? Why?

5. Which of the 10 tips did you find most challenging? Why?

6. What other tips of your own would you add to the list? Why are those tips important to you? How do you use them in your own leadership experiences?

7. Who has been the most grace-giving leader in your life? Take a moment to thank them for leading you well. Send a note, take them for coffee, or even just send an email or text.

8. This chapter also includes several next steps for your leadership journey. Make a list of two to five action steps you will commit to make in this season toward becoming a grace-giving leader. Share this list with a friend and ask them to hold you accountable.

9. As we come to the end of this journey, I want you to make it personal. This whole experience has been about getting you into a position, attitude and mindset that God can partner with and bless. How has this journey changed your life? How will you be different as a result of this experience? What will you do to share what you have learned?

10. Let's wrap this up with an exercise in thankfulness. Please make a list of all the things you gained or experienced during your study for which you are grateful. Now simply thank God for grace.

about the author

MEET JAN GREENWOOD

Jan Greenwood is a pastor, teacher, and author. This Grace-Giving Leader began leading over 30 years ago as a wife and mom. At the same time, she was always working outside her home and serving in her local church. She's held positions in the marketplace, owned her own business, been a fund-raising consultant for several Christian ministries and has even run a non-profit educational organization. She started a nonprofit of her own called More Ministries and wrote a book about healthy female relationships called **Women at War**.

While battling breast cancer, she learned so much about how to contend for your future and live beyond your circumstances that she founded **Brave Strong Girl**, an on-line mentoring community for women.

In addition to these pursuits, Jan has served in pastoral ministry since 2004. For more than a decade, she has been serving as a part of the pastoral team at Gateway Church, a multicampus church based out of the Dallas Fort Worth Metroplex that has grown to more than 100,000 active members. For several years she served in the women's ministry helping to direct a beautiful conference for women called Pink Impact. Currently, she serves as an equipping pastor where one of her most important responsibilities is to help identify, engage, and disciple the next generation of leaders. Jan and her husband Mark have been married for more than 35 years, and they have four children, Ashley, John, Luke and Matthew. They live in a suburb of Dallas.

CONNECT WITH JAN

- WEBSITE: **bravestronggirl.org**
- INSTAGRAM: **@jangreenwood**
- FACEBOOK: **jan.greenwood.16**

ALSO BY THIS AUTHOR

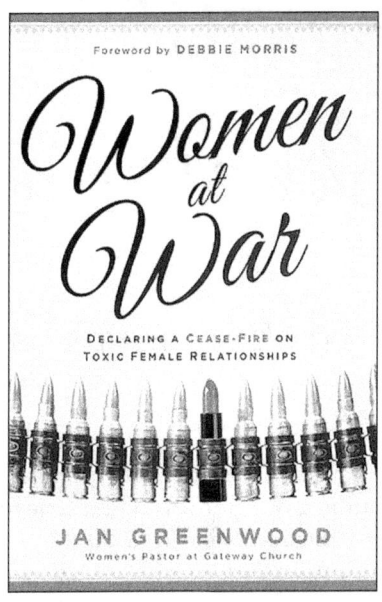

Many women have been deeply wounded by relationships with a friend, sister, or female coworker that have turned competitive, slanderous, or even vengeful. From a young age many girls experience the rejection, hurt, and mistrust that occurs when women war against one another.

Women at War will revolutionize the value women place on their own gender and the way they treat one another. Through Jan Greenwood's insightful teaching you will be inspired by important topics such as:

- Effective ways to experience healing in female relationships
- Tips and tools to turn difficult relationships into powerful ones
- How to embrace the gift of being a woman

AVAILABLE AT AMAZON.COM

> PLEASE ENJOY THIS EXCERPT FROM
> Jan Greenwood, *Women at War*
> (Lake Mary, FL: Charisma House, 2015) Used by Permission.

It's a War

WAKE UP TO THE BATTLE RAGING ALL AROUND YOU

• • •

For everything there is a season…a time to love and a time to hate, a time for war and a time for peace.
Ecclesiastes 3:1, 8, MEV

Patient is not an adjective that usually describes me. That day was no exception. As I sat in a very uncomfortable chair, I shifted my weight from one side to the other. I listened to the steps in the hallway as doctors and nurses passed by. The voices were too muffled for me to hear what they were saying. I sensed someone draw near to the door, but then they passed on by. My heart skipped a beat and my palms sweated.

I distracted myself by focusing on the clicking of the air conditioning unit and the poor choice of paint color on the wall, doing everything I could to divert my mind from the reality of where I was and the possibility of what I might hear in the next few moments. It seemed to take forever.

My thoughts drifted to the words my husband said to me just the week before when I limped into the kitchen. "Jan, if you don't get that taken care of, you won't be able to go to Egypt." He got my attention.

I love to travel, especially on mission trips. Growing up in the Bible belt, it seemed to me like everyone was a Christian and regularly attended church. I hardly knew any unbelievers. I had always heard there were many people in the world who did not know Jesus, but when I started visiting foreign countries, I saw the magnitude of the lost.

In 2009, when I heard about a mission trip to Egypt, I couldn't wait to sign up. Preparing for the trip required a tremendous amount of planning, on top of all my usual life stuff. In the end I focused so much on taking care of everything and everyone else I didn't take very good care of myself.

One day, as I sat at the conference table in my office, I experienced an intense shooting pain in my hip. For a couple of weeks, every time I'd get up or down, my hip hurt. It got better but then got worse again. The pain became so bad I couldn't wear high heels, and I started dragging my leg a little bit.

But I can be hardheaded sometimes. Only at Mark's insistence, and with the threat of missing the trip to Egypt, did I stop and give the matter some attention.

> **Women have been fighting to be who they are for centuries, especially when they find themselves in situations and circumstances that leave them feeling stripped of their femininity.**

I made an appointment with an orthopedist. Two days after seeing him, I went in for an MRI of my hip.

A week later Mark and I returned to get my test results. The doctor opened his computer and showed us the MRI. He pointed at a portion of my hip and explained the tissue was soft and expanding, which was indicative of a possible tumor.

Tumor? My husband and I stared at him, and then at each other, both of us speechless.

The following Monday I went to the hospital for more tests. During a bone scan, the nurse casually asked, "When was the last time you had a mammogram?"

Over the past several years I'd scheduled a mammogram three times; all three times I cancelled the appointment due to my overbooked calendar. (Maybe you can relate. Sometimes I get so busy taking care of others I forget to take care of myself.) Her comment frightened me and tears began to slip down my face. I quietly mumbled something in return, not wanting to let her know how her comment impacted me.

When I finished the scan I was whisked down the hall to radiology for a mammogram and ultrasound. Then I was escorted to that uncomfortable chair in that ugly room I mentioned earlier where I waited alone to see what the consequences would be for overlooking my health.

I AM WOMAN

When I was a teenager, my dad bought me a bright yellow minibike. We lived in the country where the mailbox was a mile away, the nearest neighbor was down the road and around the corner, and I was more likely to see a cow than a human any day of the week. That little motorcycle gave me freedom to go places and to do things I would never have been able to do without it.

One day as I drove my minibike down the road to visit a friend, wind whipping my hair every which way, I pulled back the throttle and sang at the top of my lungs the Helen Reddy song "I Am Woman."

At this point in my life I had no idea what it meant to be a woman, but I identified with the powerful declarations in those lyrics.

Women often feel the need to declare their femininity. To own it. To fight for it.

I pondered the parallel between that battle and the one I faced in the waiting room that day. Women have been fighting to be who they are for centuries, especially when they find themselves in situations and circumstances that leave them feeling stripped of their femininity.

I snapped out of my memories and back to the moment as I sat in the chair. My heart cried out, *"I am woman! Don't take that away from me!"*

Finally, the radiologist arrived and my fears were realized. "Mrs. Greenwood, you have stage IV breast cancer, and it's metastasized to your hip."

My world spun out of control. I felt weak. Stunned. Shattered.

I knew enough about cancer to understand what I was facing. Cancer would try to steal my femininity, waging an assault on my body, which would threaten the core of who I was. Chemotherapy would sap my strength and expose me to a variety of frightening consequences. It would cause my hair to fall out. Surgical intervention would mean losing one or both of my breasts. My natural strength and zeal for life would be tempered by fatigue and worry. In one fell swoop, I would be bereft of the things that most identified me as a woman. But even more fearful than the effect on my appearance was the very real threat I might die.

I had been attacked—blindsided really—by a vicious, insidious foe that was trying to take my life as the "spoils of war."

THE GREAT I AM

Within a week of my diagnosis I endured a battery of additional tests and procedures. Two weeks after the diagnosis, I began chemotherapy.

I had become a *patient*.

> It became clear my deepest desire would be to leave them a legacy of love.

Not long after my first round of chemo, Mark and I went to a church service. Everyone else stood for worship. I felt so tired and overwhelmed I just sat there.

I closed my eyes, and suddenly it was as if I had entered a room where Jesus was waiting for me.

In my frustration, fatigue, fear, and anger, I confronted Him. "Are You really like this? Are You harsh? Is this some kind of punishment?"

He didn't respond but just kept looking at me with compassion while I vented.

When I finally ran out of steam, I became silent. After a few tense moments I asked the true question on my heart. "Are You going to heal me?"

"I Am," He responded.

I knew what He was saying. Not just "I am going to heal you." He spoke His name to me and revealed His character—the Great I Am. Reminding me who He is, He was saying, "No matter what, Jan, I am enough."

His calm response settled me. Hope began to flicker. In a moment, with my anger and desperation poured out, His peace enveloped me. The weight of His words wrapped around me like a blanket—the Comforter—surrounding my soul. I began to believe God was going to heal me. I knew "I Am" would be with me every step of the way. It was enough.

THE BATTLE FOR WOMANHOOD

I began an intensive year and a half of aggressive treatments—and a lifelong assignment to pursue, apprehend, and maintain my health. After nineteen rounds of chemotherapy, a lumpectomy, and a full round of radiation therapy, God did heal me. I am well.

Coming face-to-face with my mortality changed my perspective and my priorities. Mark and I gave serious consideration to the value we place on family, faith, and friends. I needed to measure my days and carefully consider what my legacy would be.

During the treatment process, I often looked into the faces of my children, feeling the depth of my love for them.

If I could only do a few things before my death, what would I choose? What would my last words be? What treasure would I bestow on them?

It became clear my deepest desire would be to leave them a legacy of love.

I held my children in my arms and told them, "I love you." I asked them to forgive me for the times I'd caused them pain. I talked about the faithfulness of our God and assured them of His willingness to heal all our hurts—physical, emotional, and spiritual.

But I decided I wouldn't stop there. I would start a revolution of love that would go beyond my own children and reach women everywhere. For years the Lord had been teaching me about the battle raging for our femininity and our relationships. He had been speaking to me about the power of love to restore them. I wanted to share what I'd learned while exposing the threats, lies, and wounds women impose on one another—first for the benefit of my daughter, Ashley…and then for my future daughters-in-law…and finally for all the women I love, even for those I didn't personally know.

WINNING THE WAR

I wish I could tell you I was spared the ravages of my war against cancer or give you a story of instant healing without suffering. The truth is I experienced grueling negative side effects from my chemotherapy treatment. My hair fell out, challenging my self-esteem. I had to surrender the diseased portion of my breast to surgery and faced terrible battles with fear. I walked with a painful limp for a long time, and it has taken me years to regain my physical strength. I didn't get to make the trip to Egypt that was so important to me, and I tasted the disappointment of lost opportunity.

But I have won some major battles along the way. In the process of walking through this frightening season, I overcame not only cancer but also many of my fears, wounds, and insecurities. I found the courage to fight for my womanhood on both the natural and the supernatural fields. I discovered I am eternally secure in the hands of a loving, warring Savior who proves His faithfulness to me over and over. I have retained my femininity and embraced its power. I now know who I am is only superficially related to my physical appearance.

Now when I hear or say, "I am," it gives me a boost of strength as I recall God's message to me of His love and power. Every day I remind myself, "I am well. I am woman."

The same God who championed me through my struggle with cancer can bring about victory in the war for our femininity as well. I now know no disease, weapon, or wound can steal who we are. Our enemy is strong, but this battle does not have to overwhelm us. Let me assure you, we are on the winning side. When women come together, united in love, we are powerful.

• • •

QUESTIONS FOR REFLECTION

Maybe you've been in a battle similar to mine. Maybe it hasn't been a fight for your health, but rather a fight for your family or your values or your faith. I'd like you to consider your own story as you begin these first moments of reflection. Think about your journey—where you began and how far you've come. From this position we will begin to dig a little deeper into your perspective on your gender and the female relationships all around you. Now is a good time to open your journal and begin to record your experiences and thoughts.

> What does "femininity" mean to you? What does it mean to be a woman?

> Describe one or two of the most important female relationships in your life. Are/Were these positive or negative experiences? Why?

> Describe a moment or a season when you began to realize there was a war among women. What was happening in your life?

> How did you respond to those circumstances? How did you respond to God in those circumstances? Take a minute to process this moment or this season with God.

Let's pause here and ask God some questions. Maybe this is a new way of communicating with God. He loves to speak to His daughters to tell us the truth about how He sees us and loves us. Just stop for a moment and get quiet. Don't be afraid; He's a good God. He's gentle and kind, and He loves you very much. He speaks in thoughts or in pictures, and sometimes in just an impression. Listen.

God, what lies have I believed about me as a woman?

What lies have I believed about my femininity?

What is the truth about me? About my femininity?

Write down what you hear. (This would be a great moment to make your first entry in your journal.) If it makes you feel yucky or ashamed, it's not God. On the other hand, if it makes you feel loved and valued, it most assuredly is God!

Take what He said about you and your femininity and declare it! Write it down or even share it. Boldly declare the truth of what God says about who you are!

AVAILABLE AT AMAZON.COM

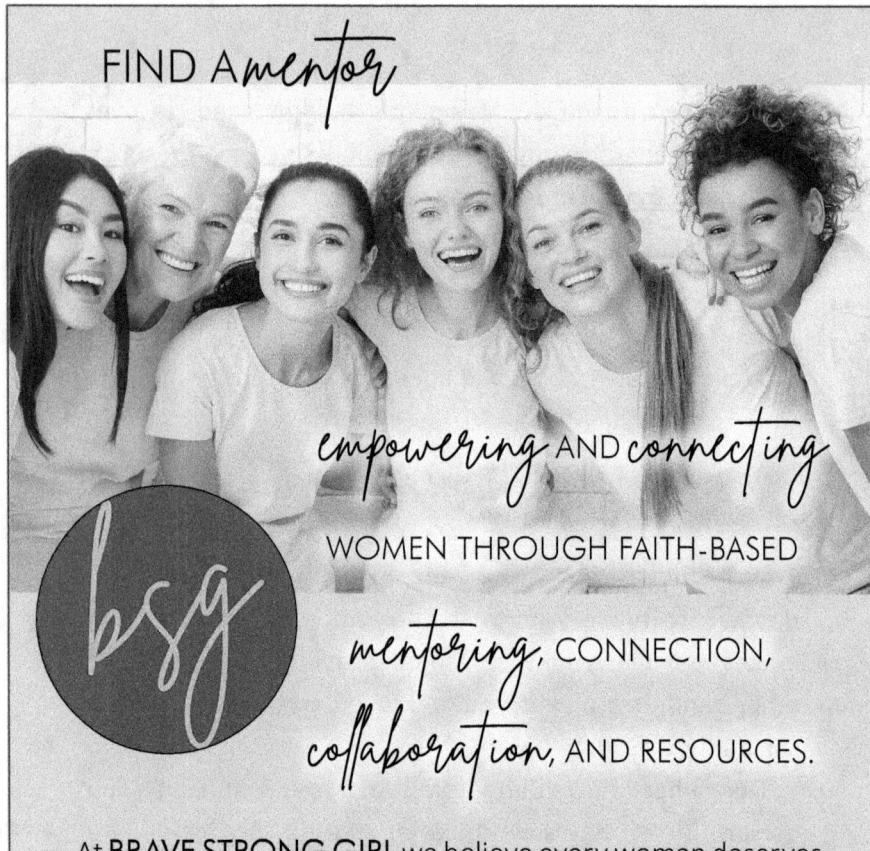

www.ingramcontent.com/pod-product-compliance
Lightning Source LLC
LaVergne TN
LVHW051517070426
835507LV00023B/3153